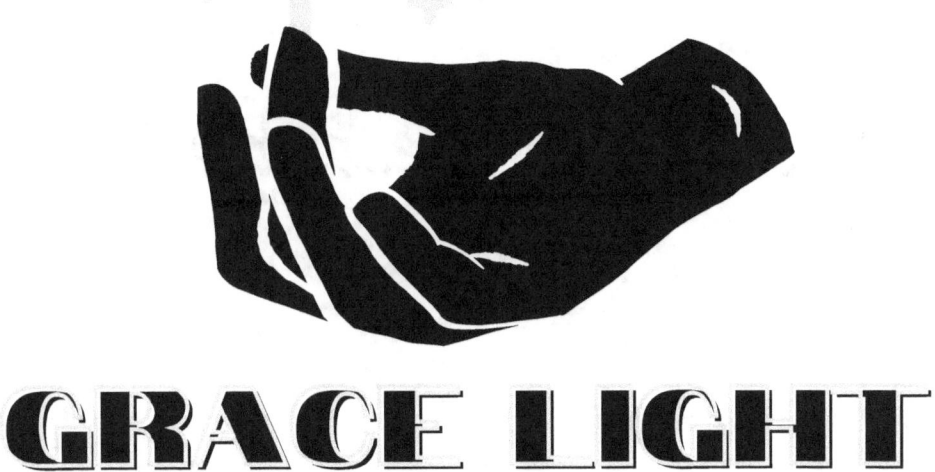

GRACE LIGHT

1 Corinthians 16:23 (KJV)

The grace of our Lord Jesus Christ be with you.

Copyright © 2020 Grace Light
All Rights Reserved.

No part of this publication may be copied or reproduced in any format, by any means, including electronic methods, without the prior written permission of the publisher of this book.

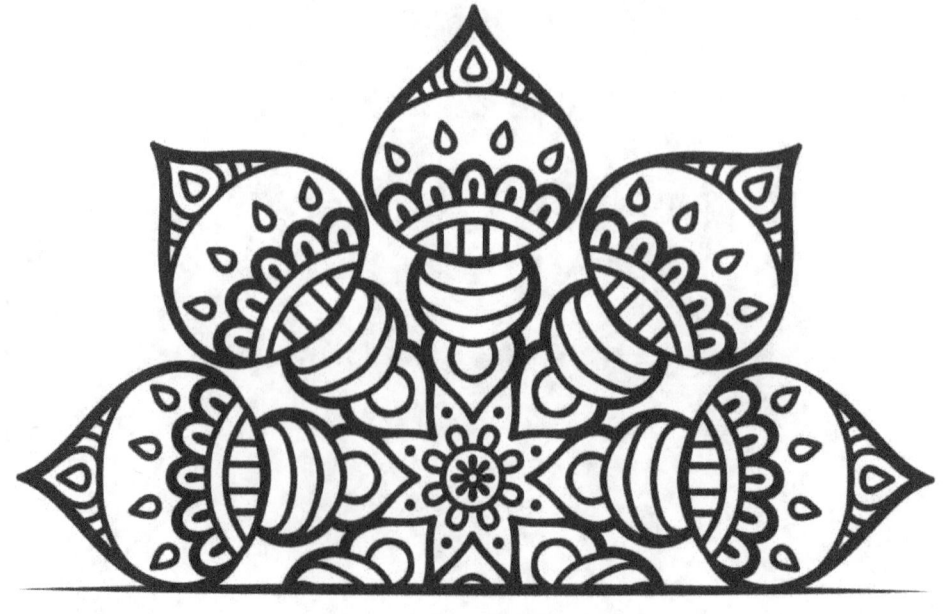

This Book Belongs To:

_____

_____

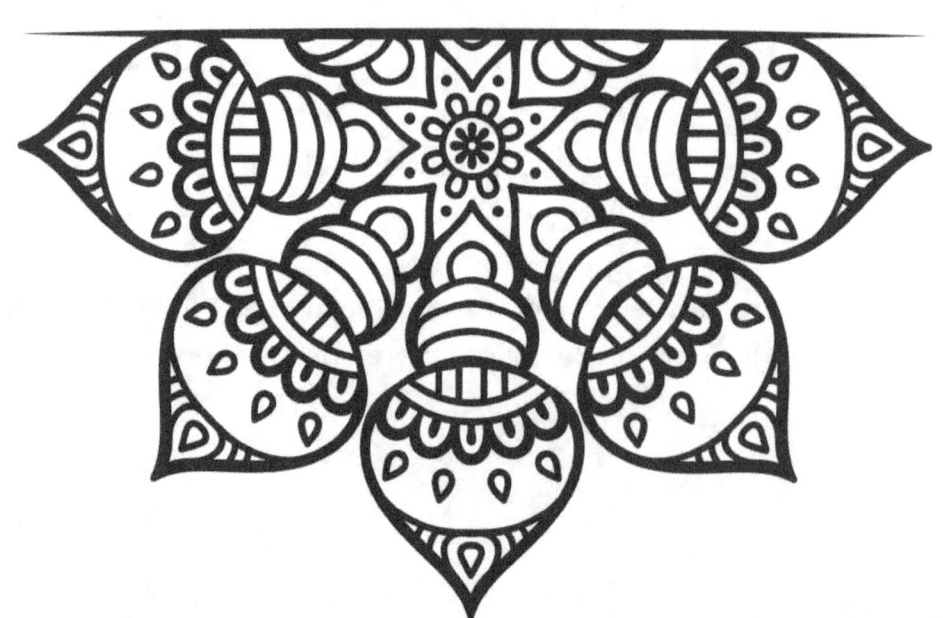

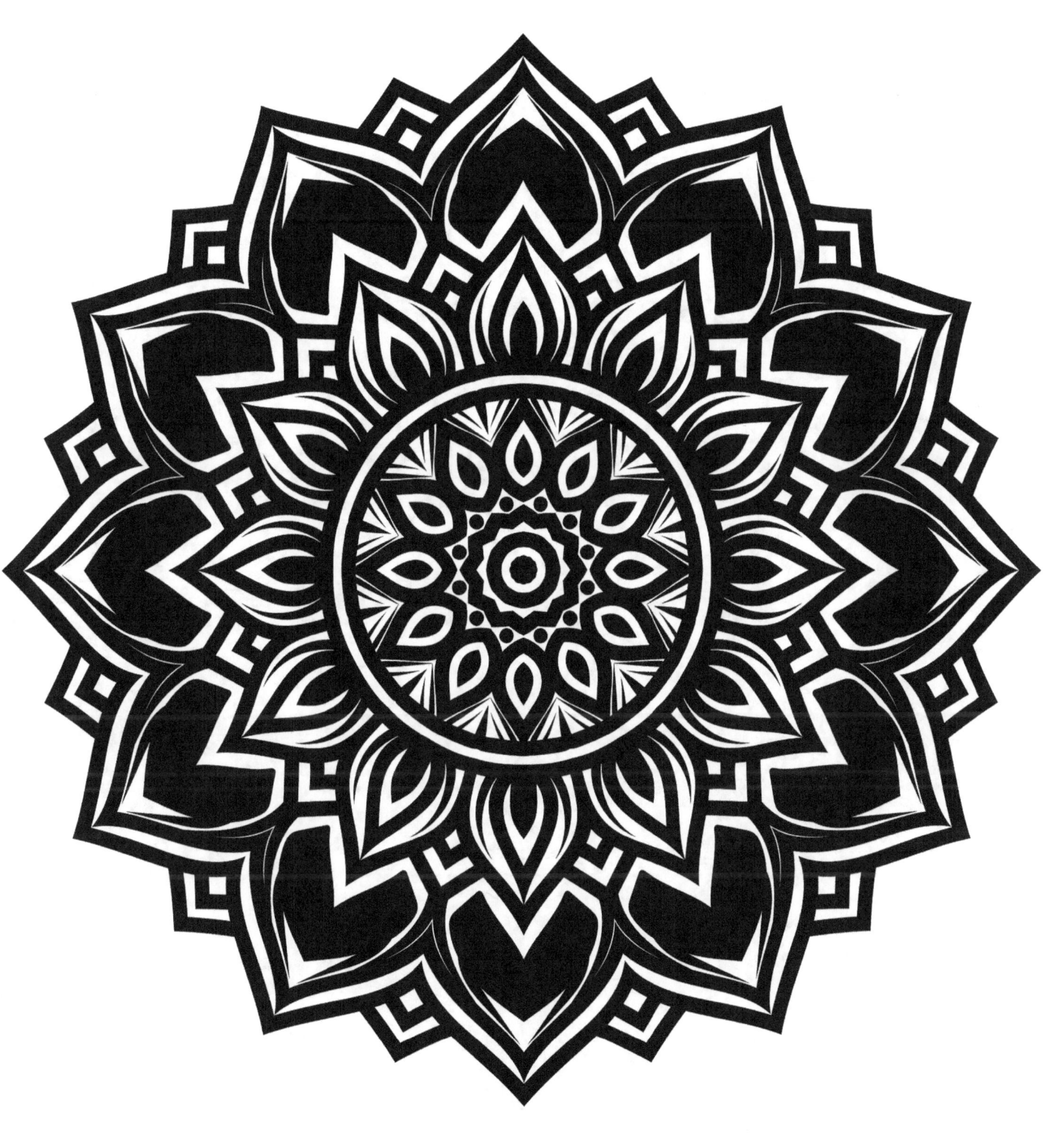

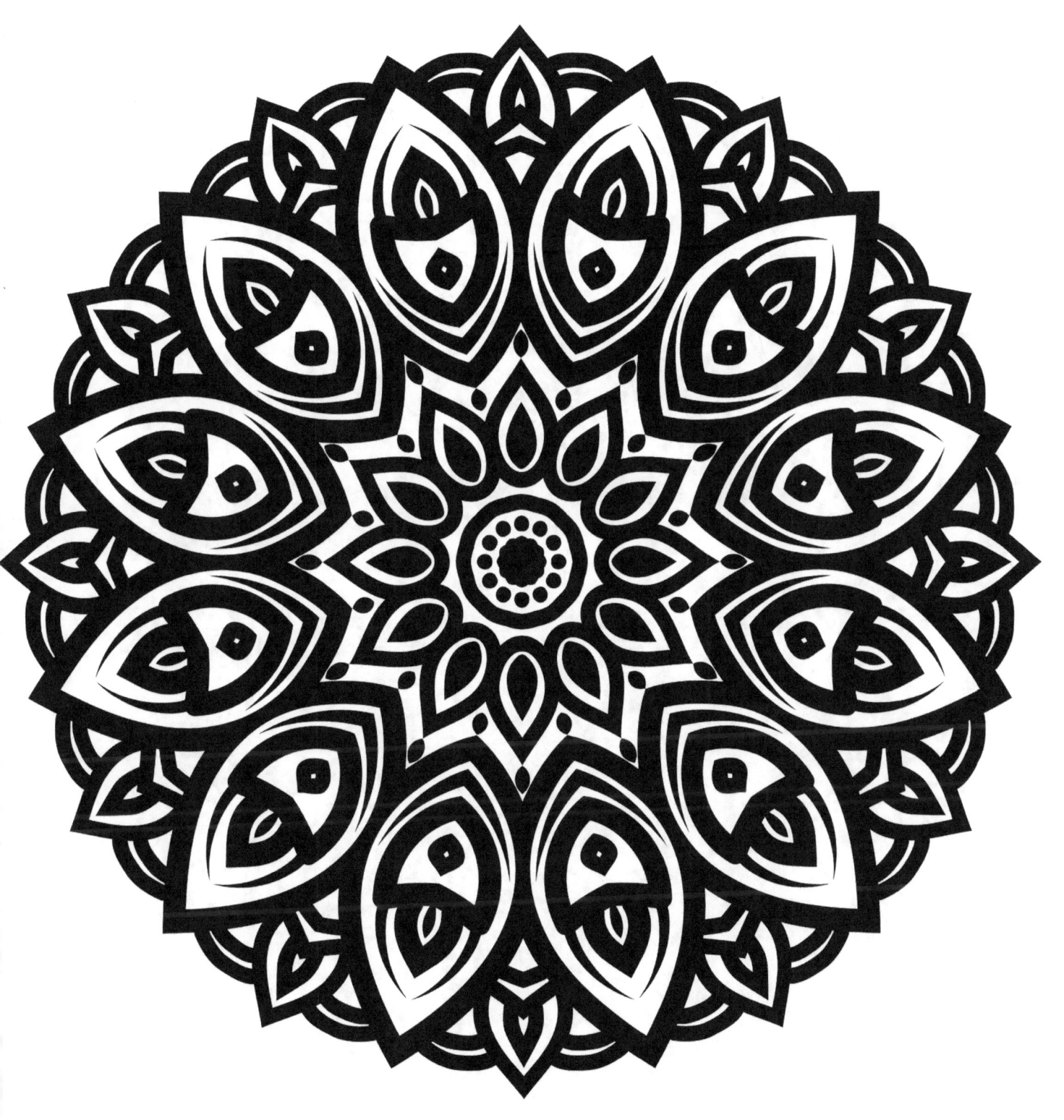

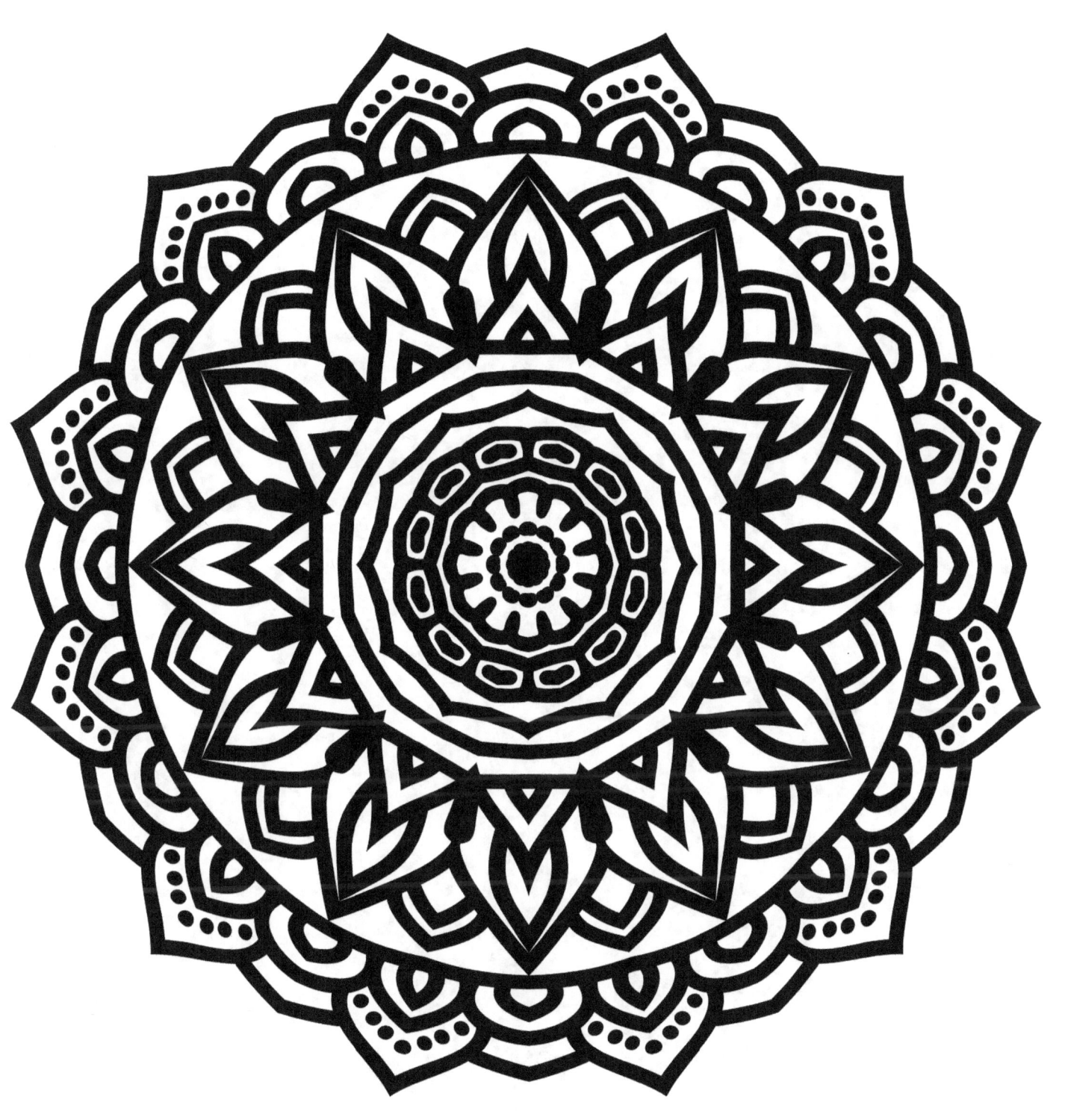

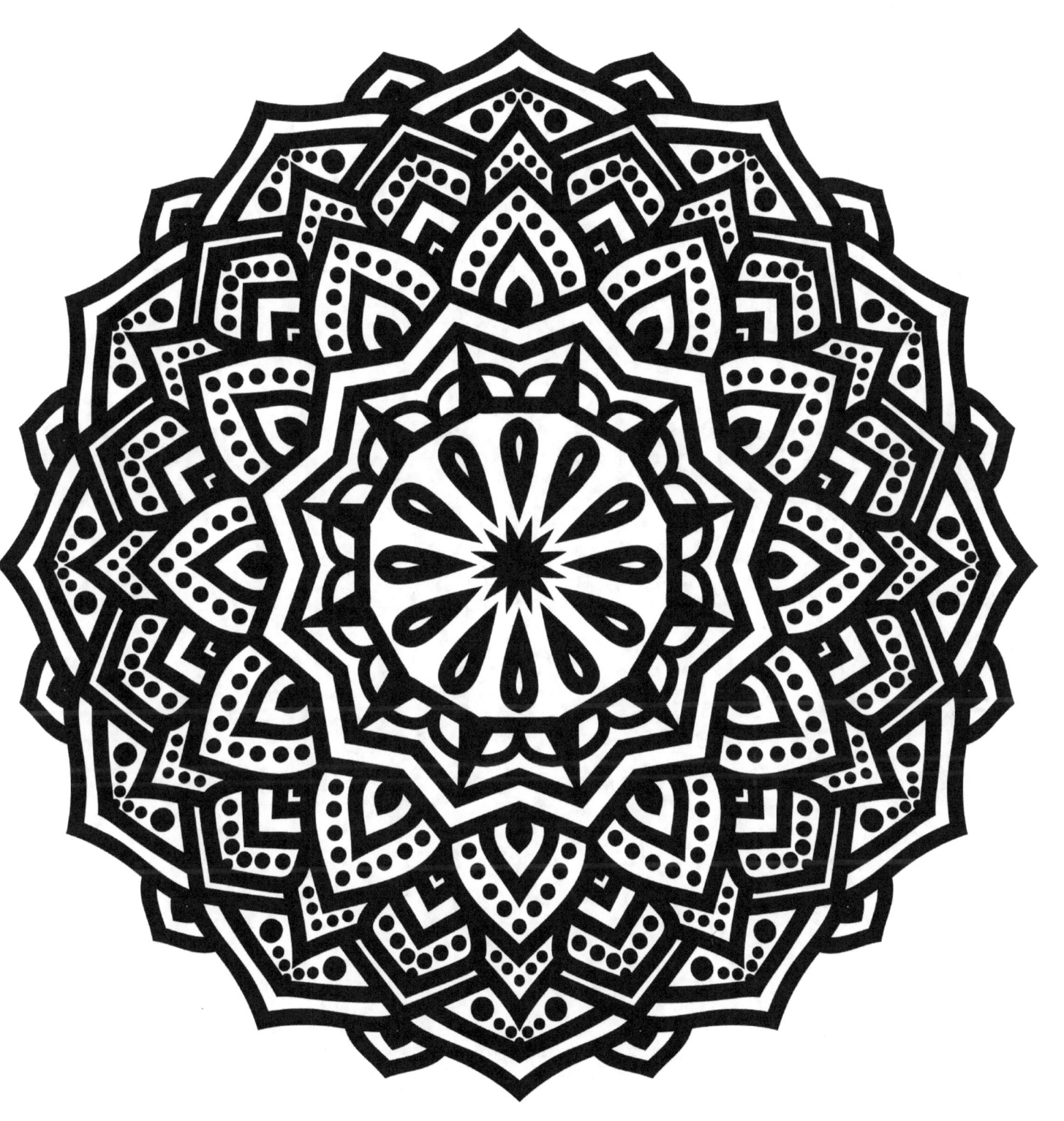

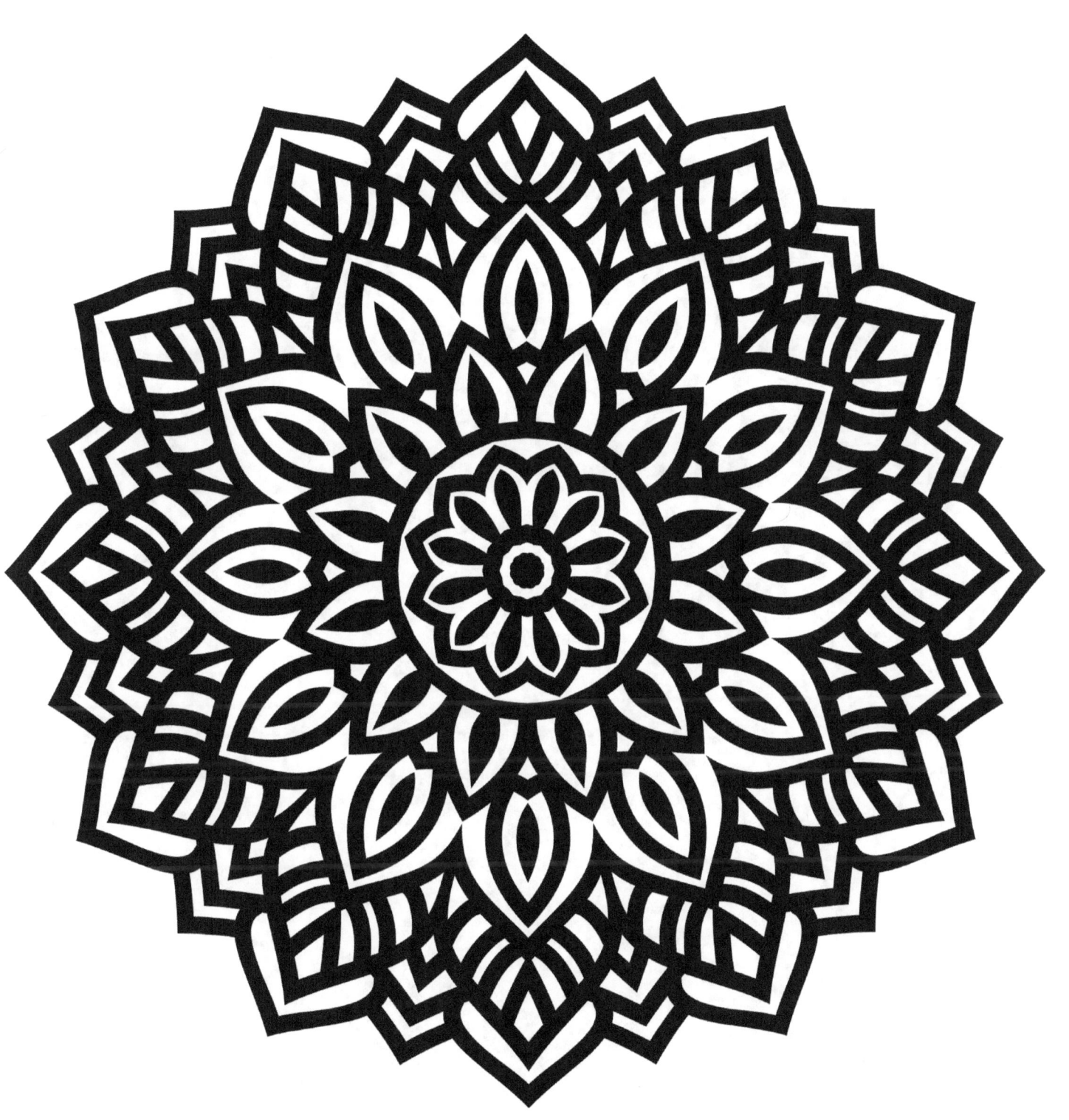

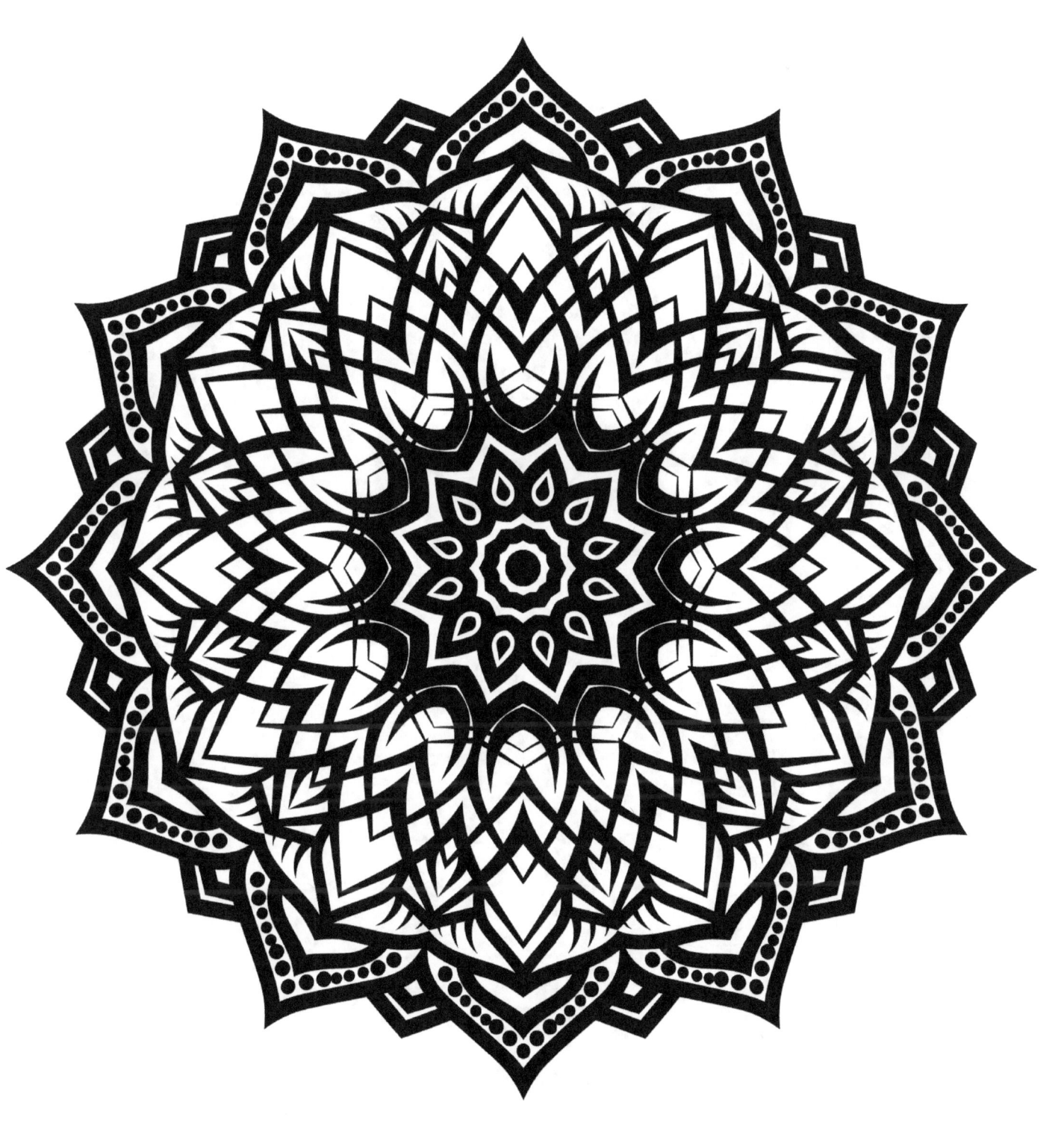

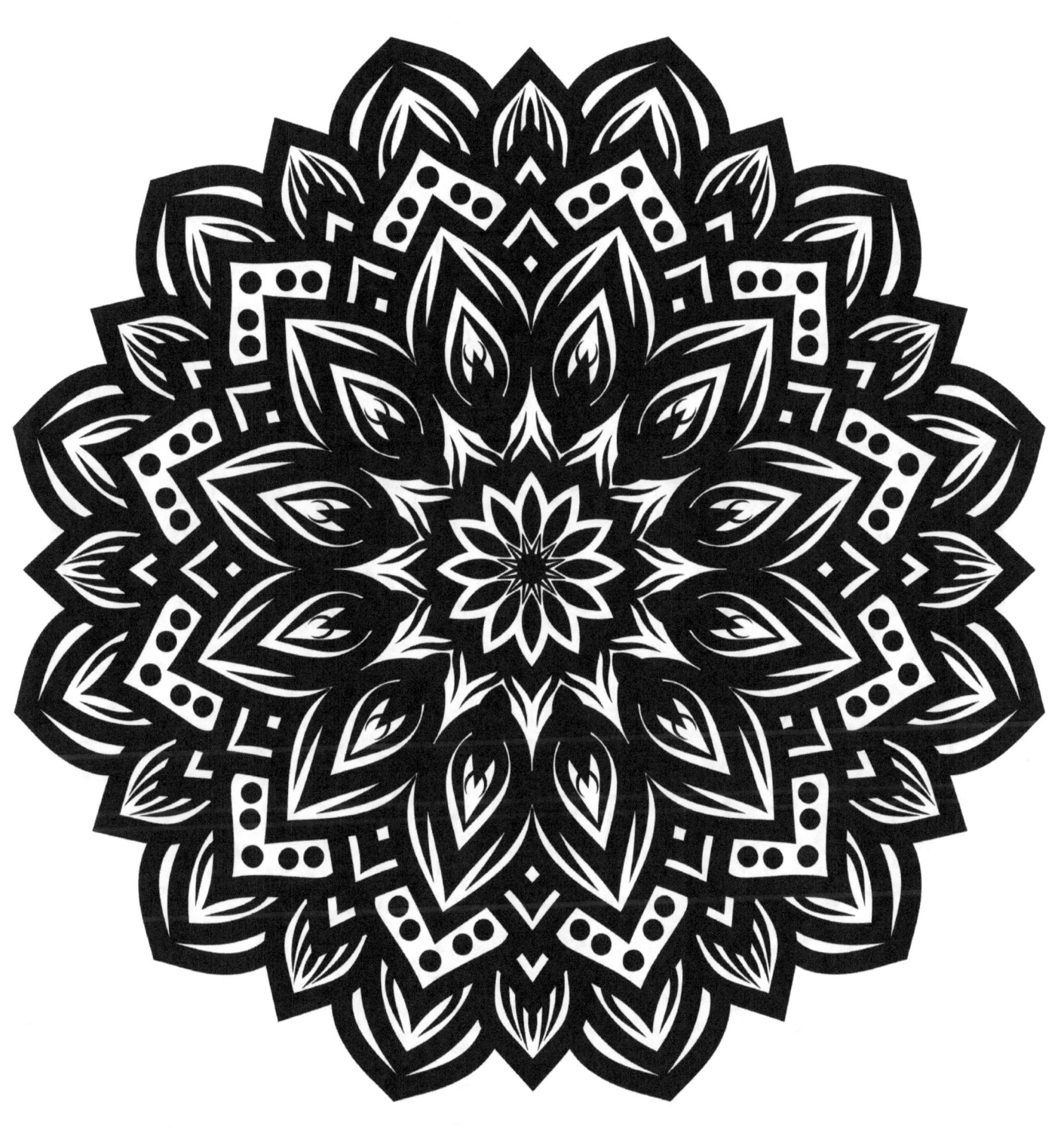

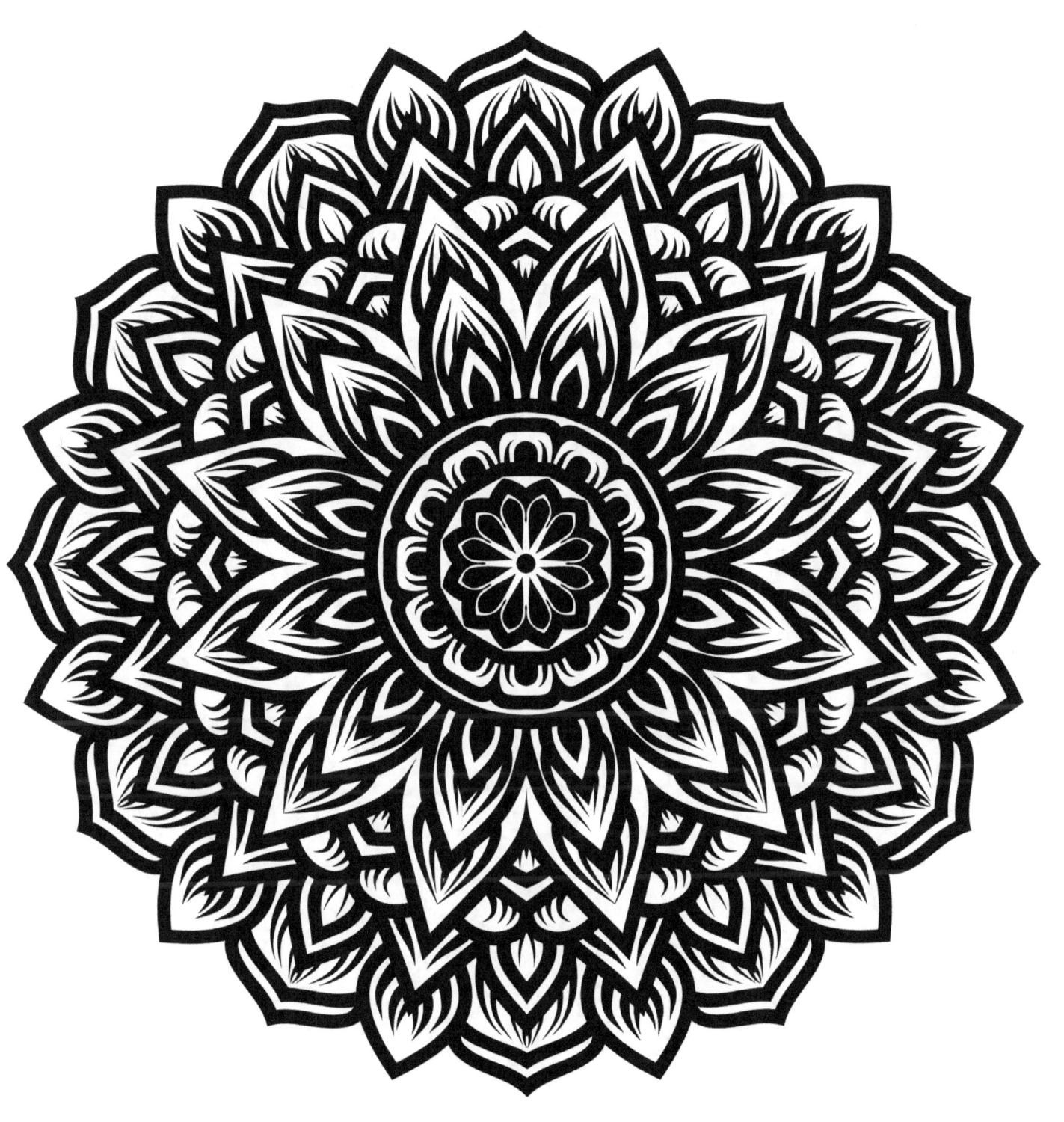

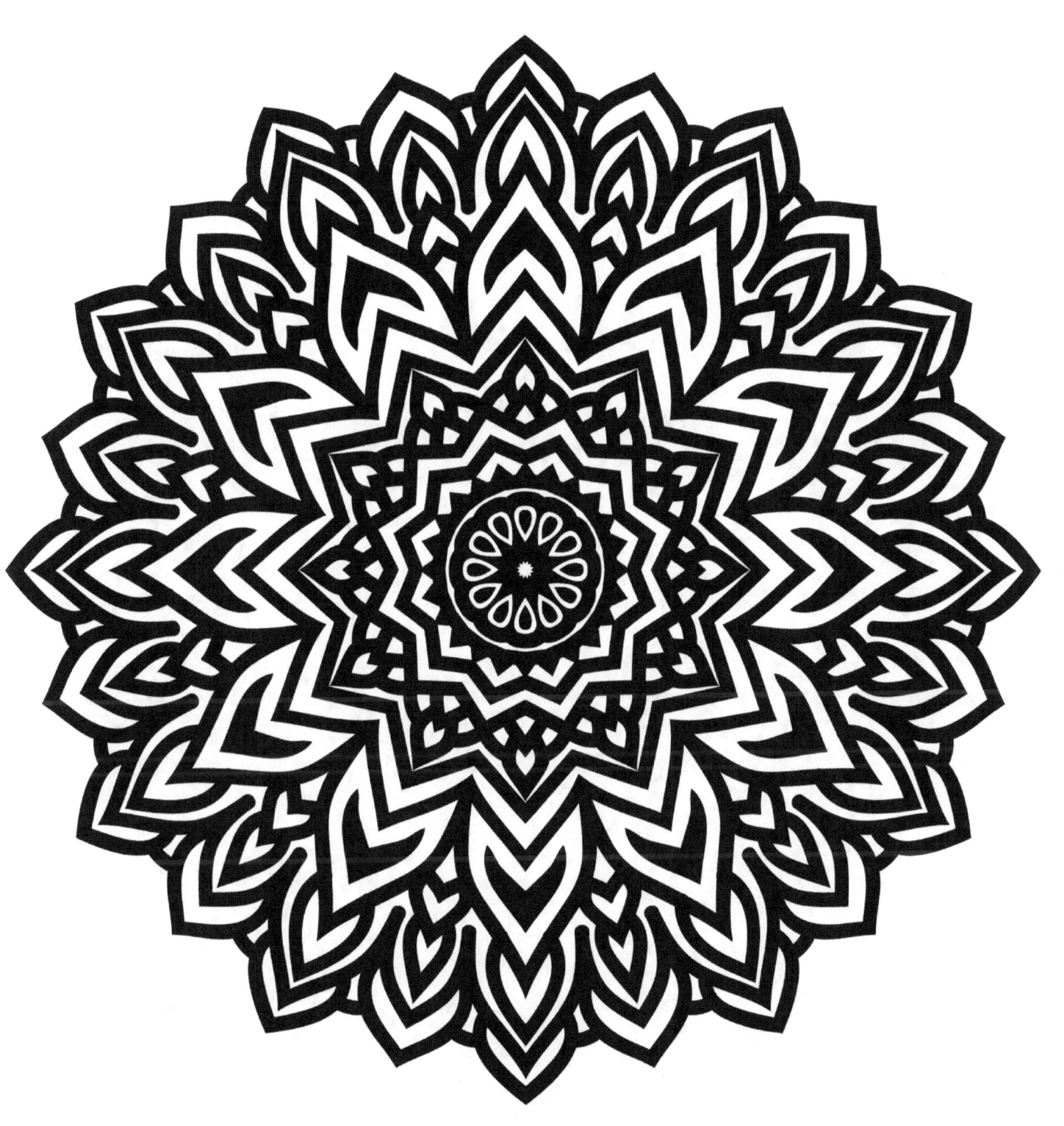

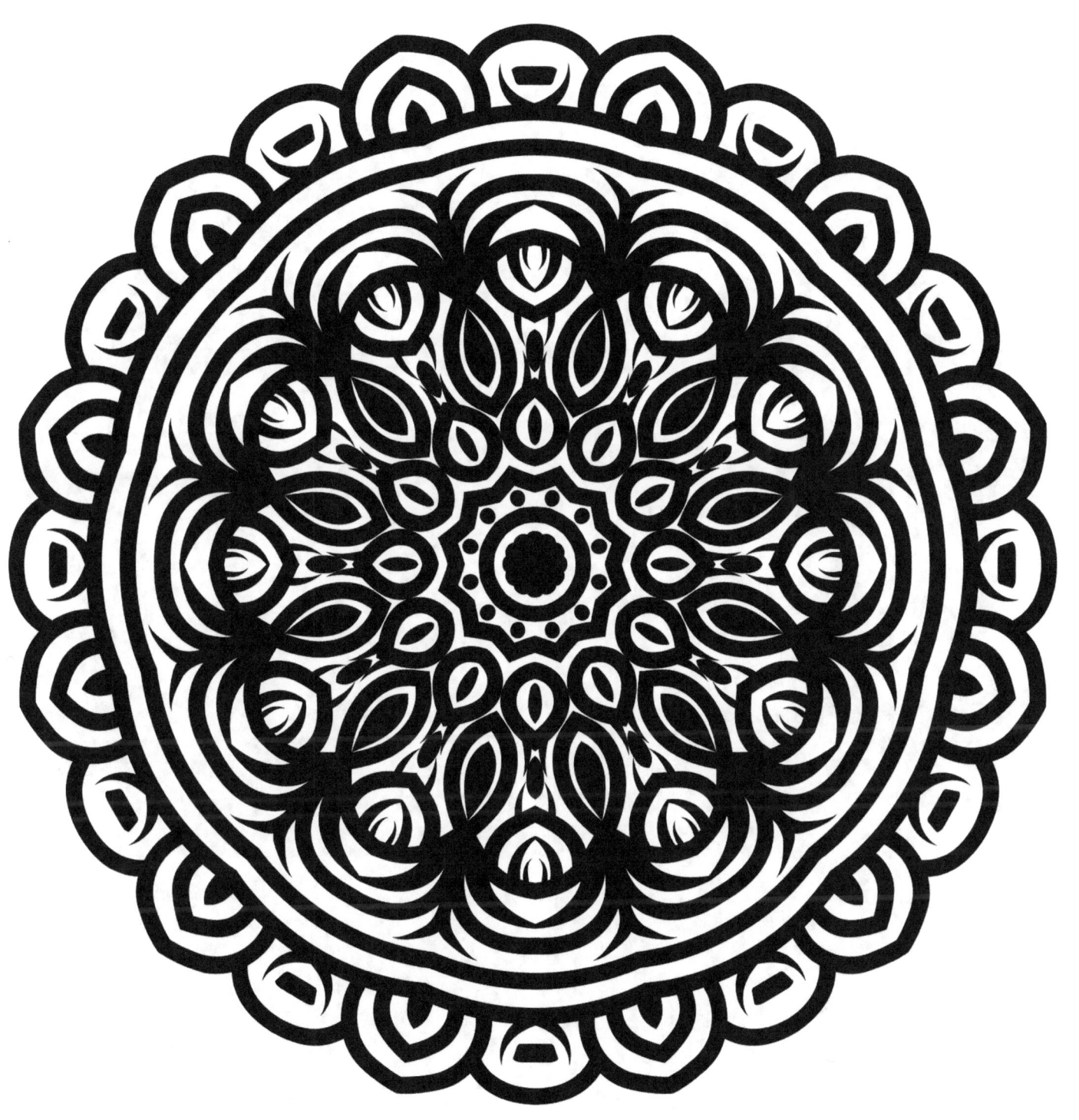

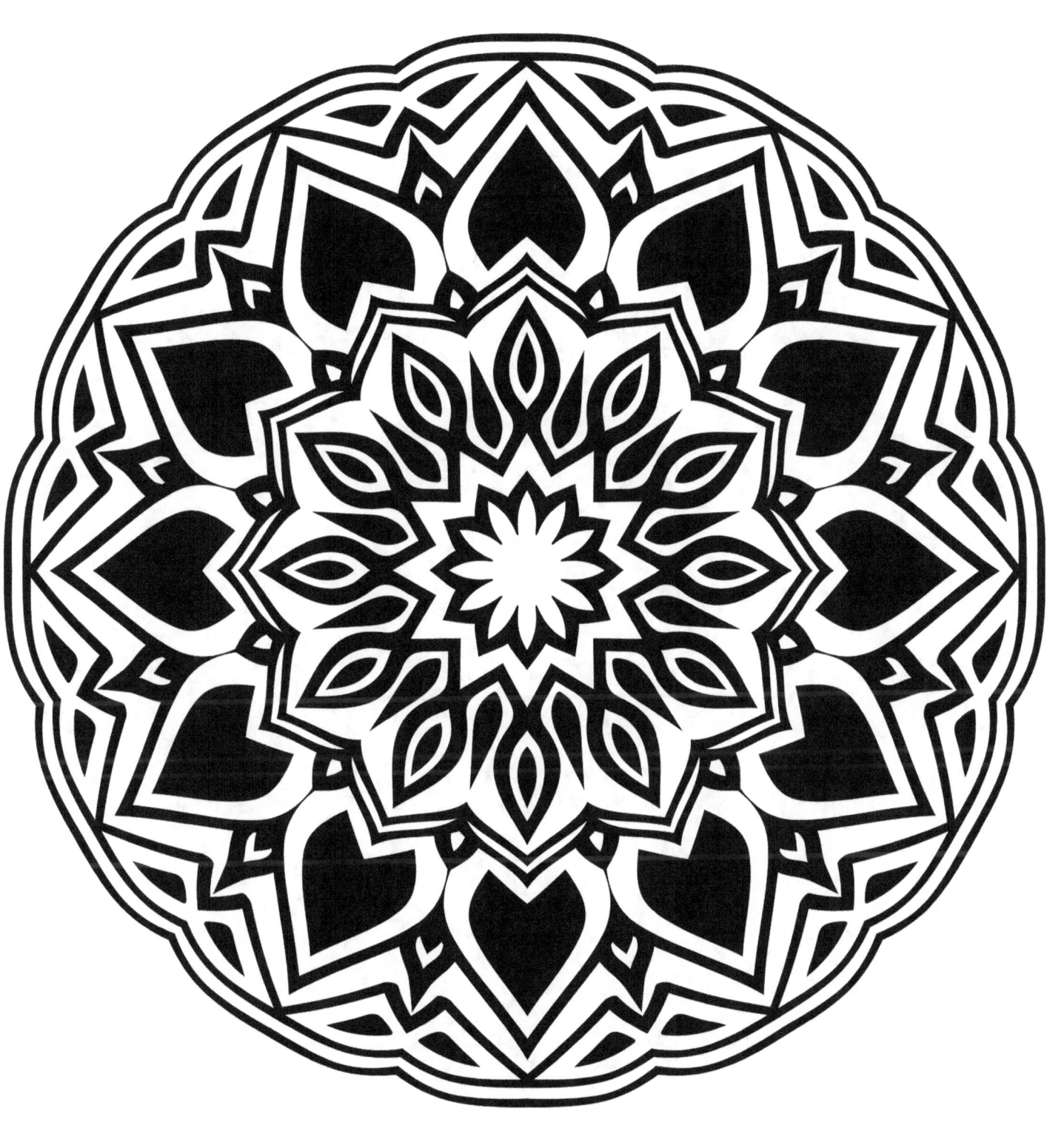

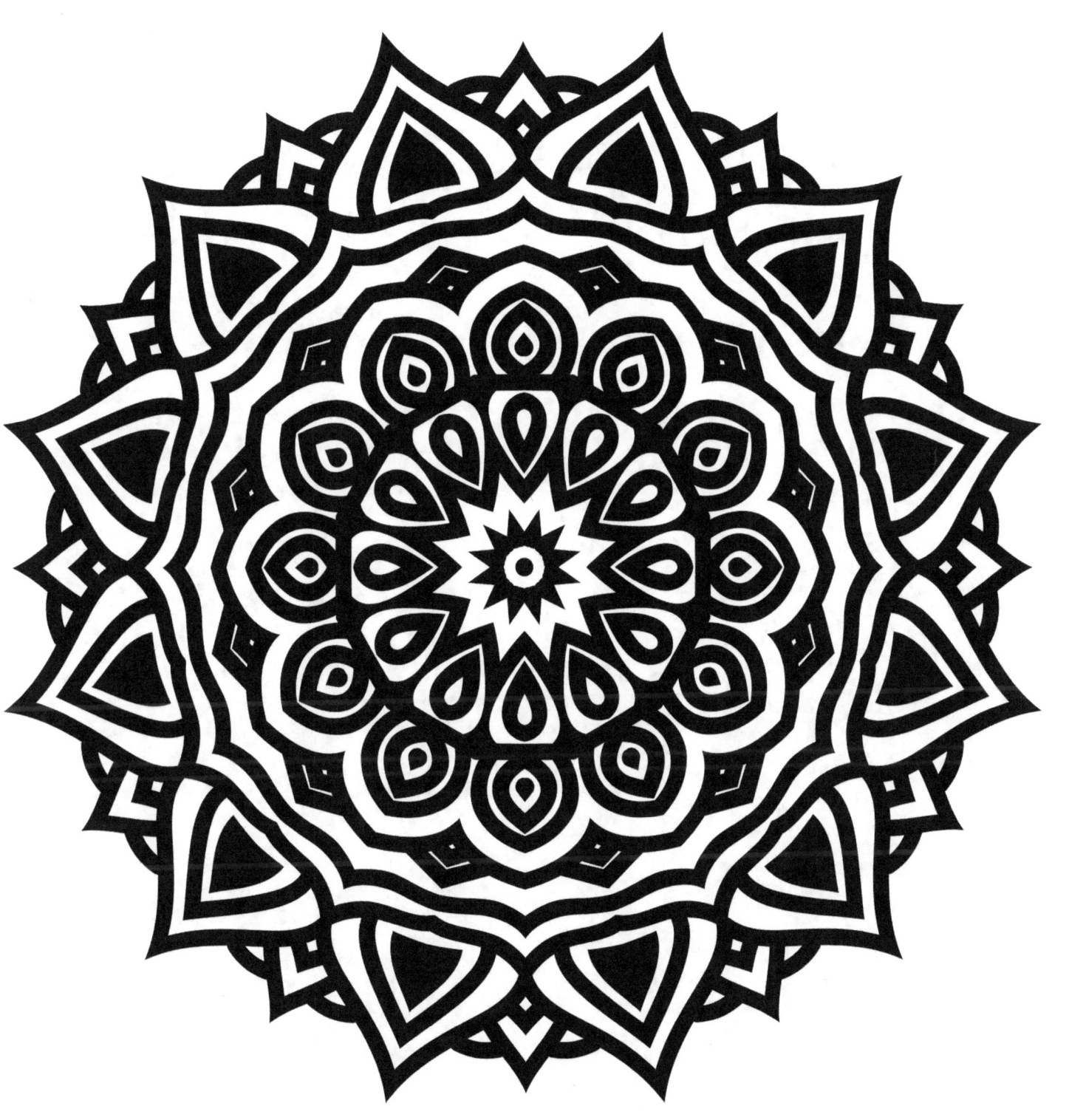

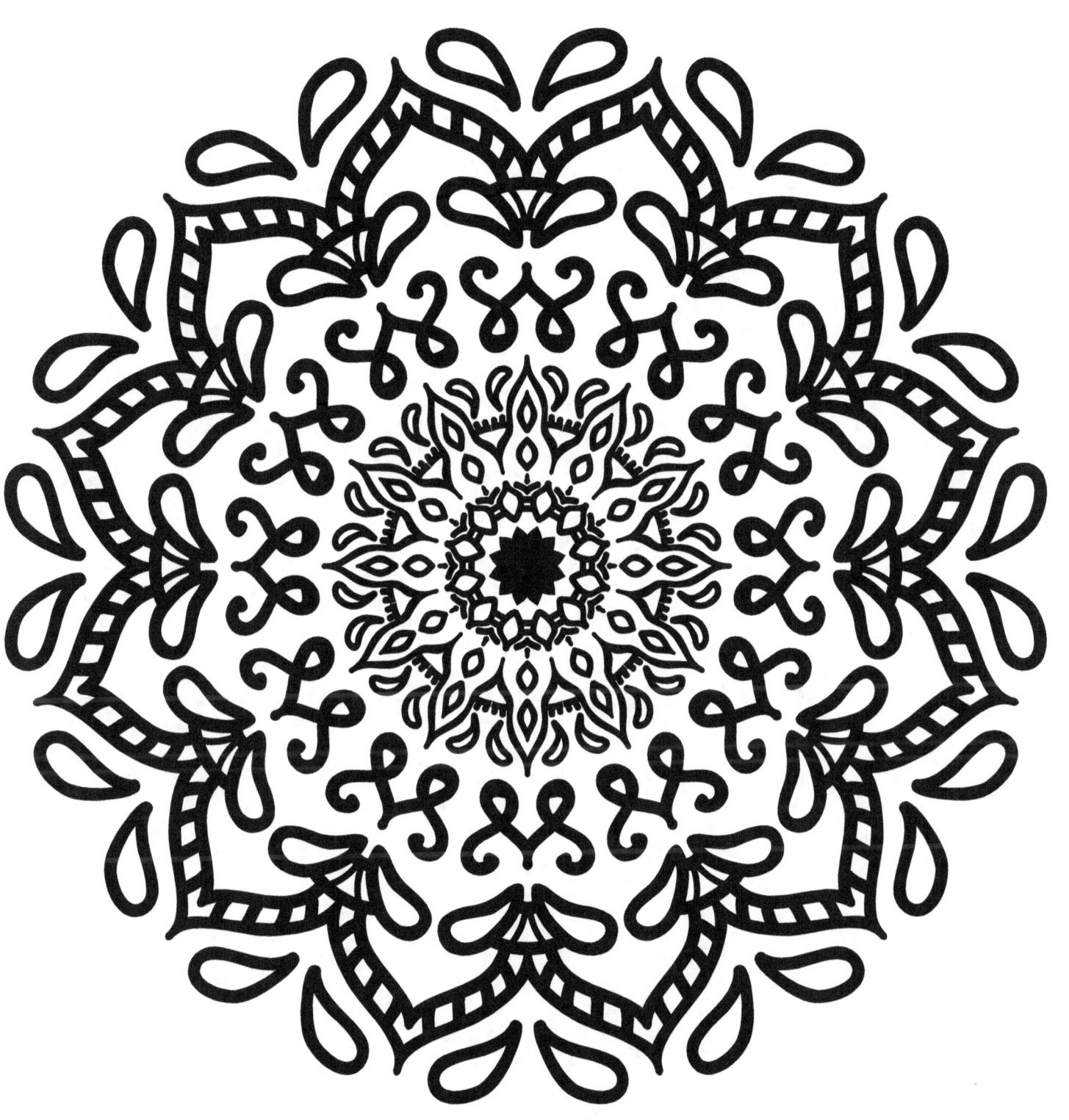

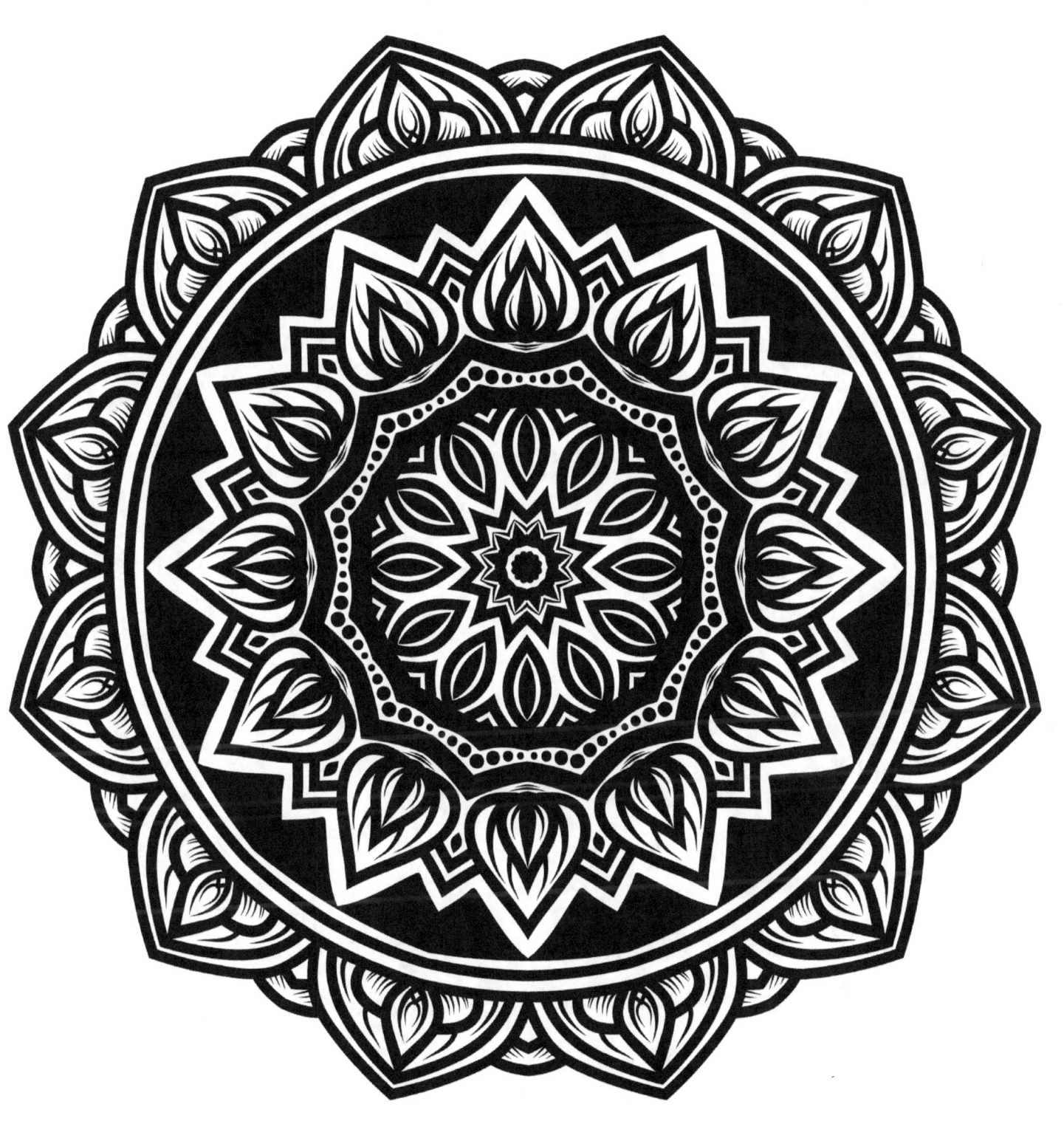

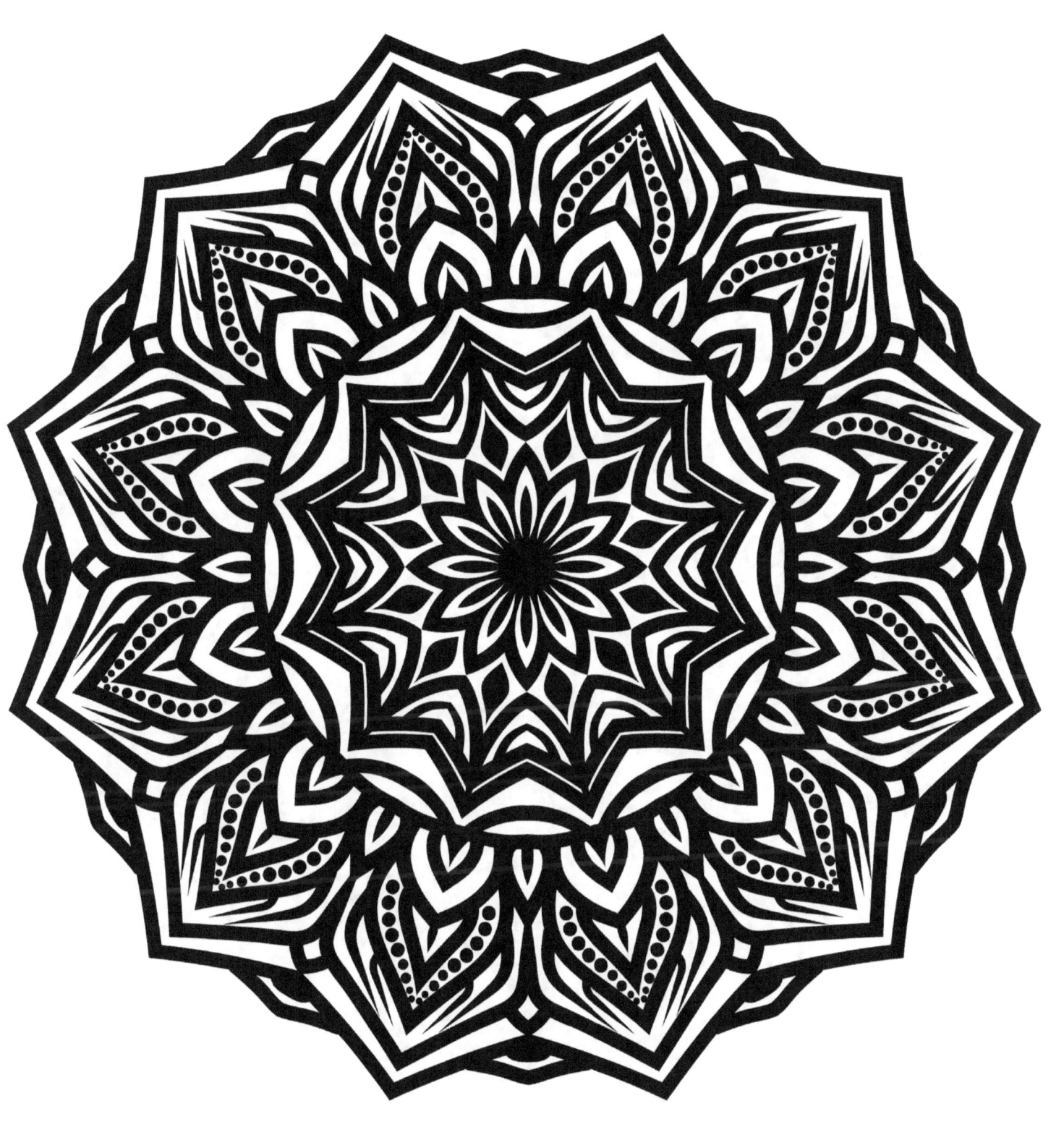

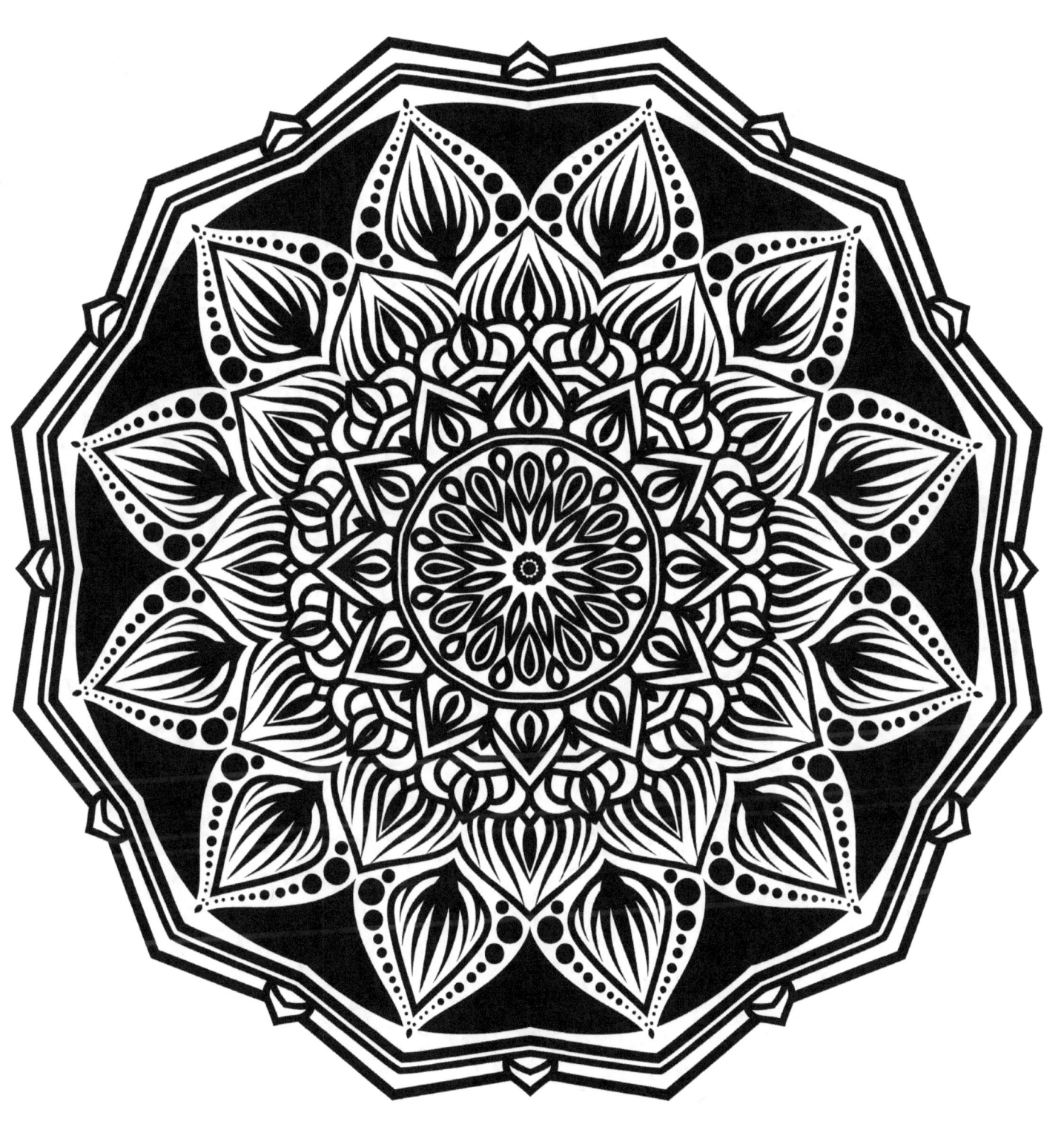

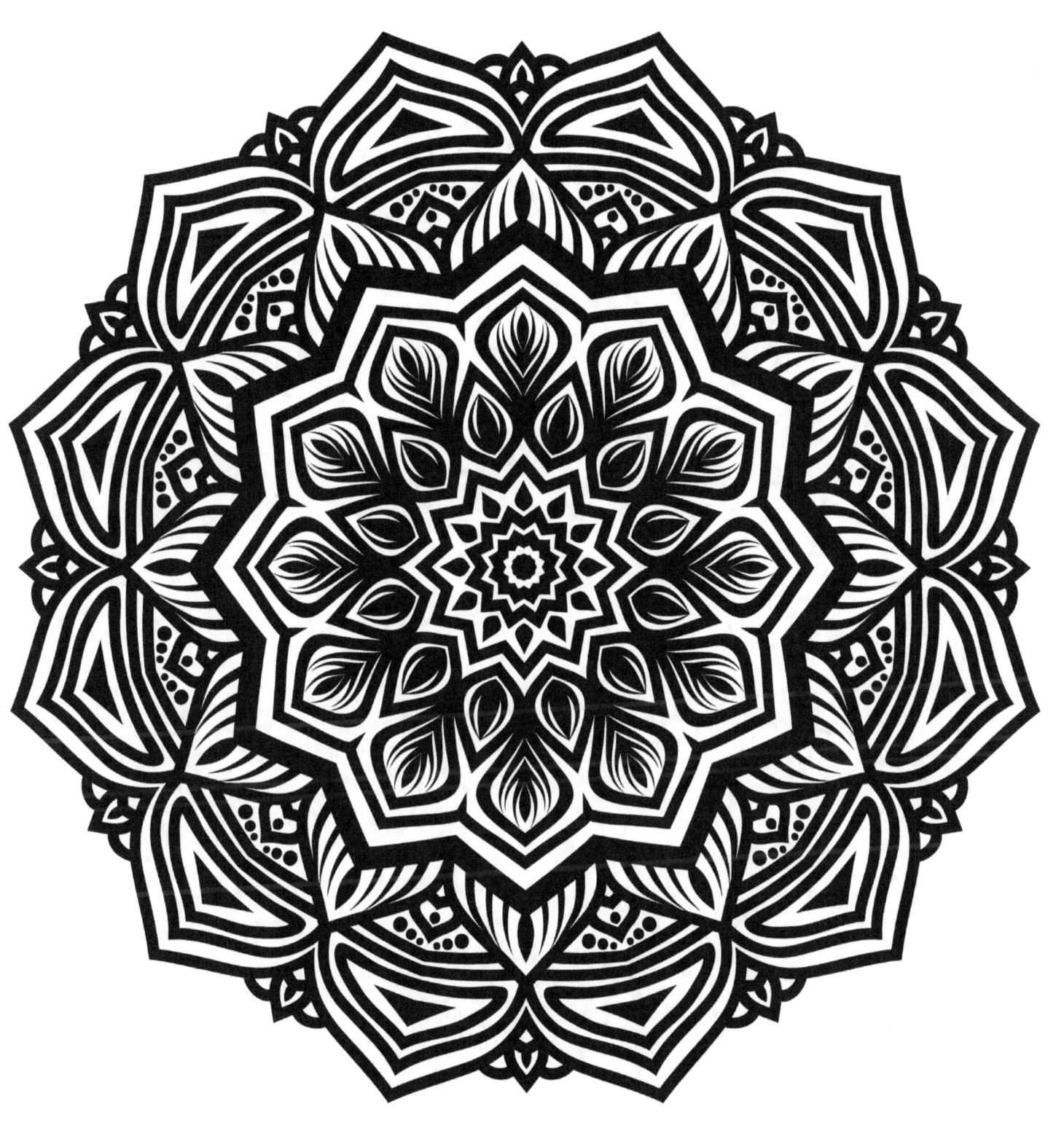

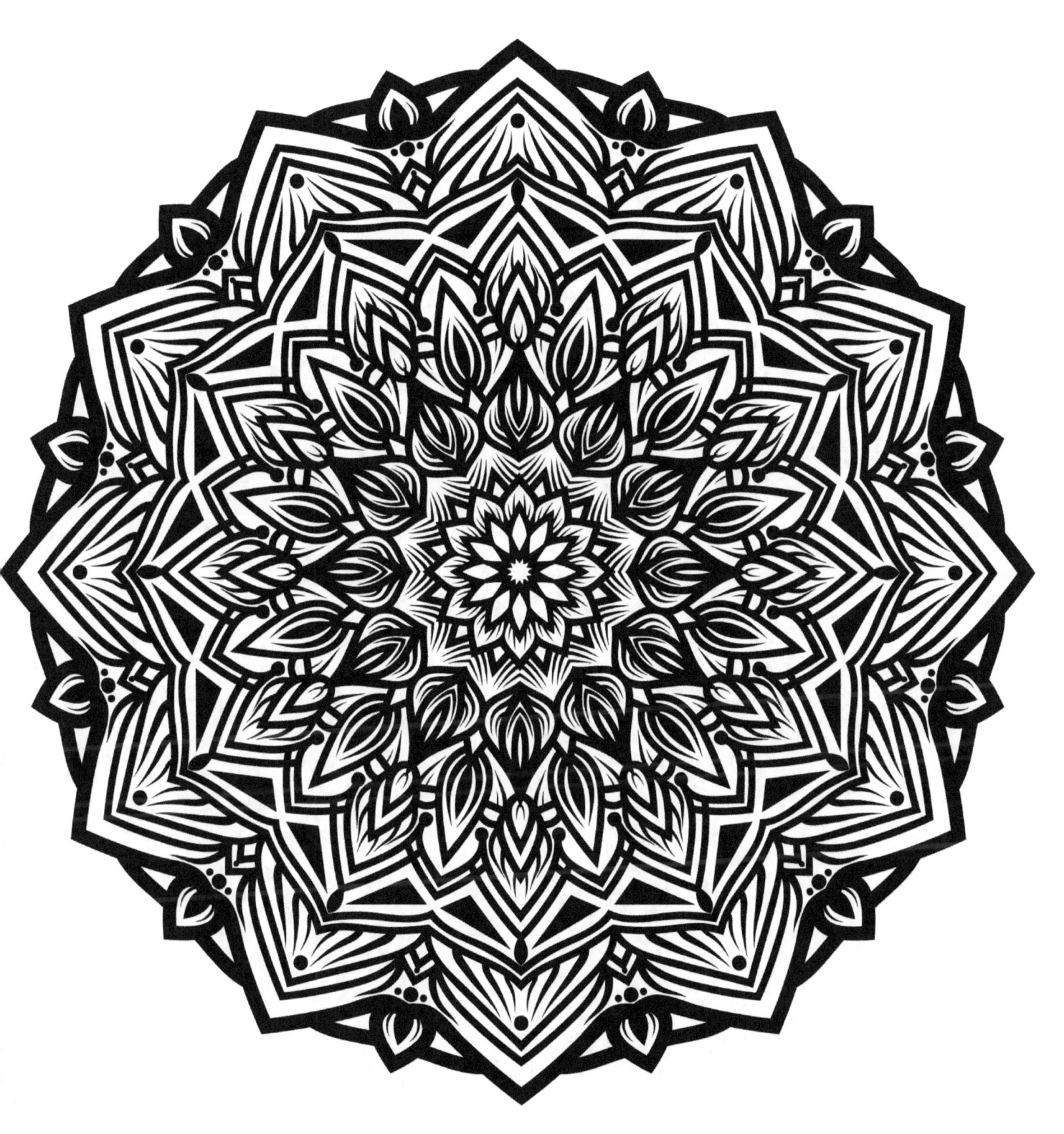

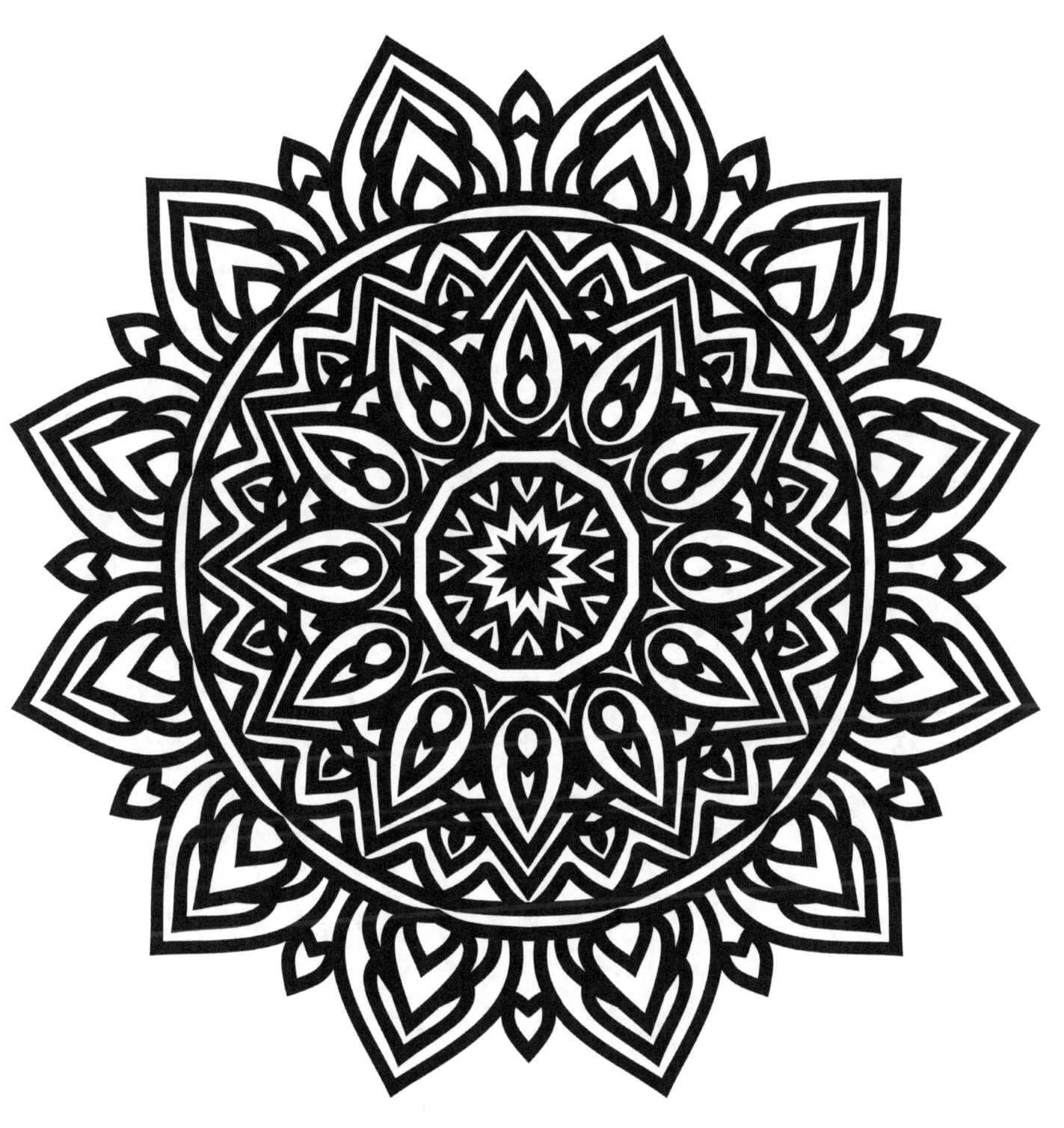

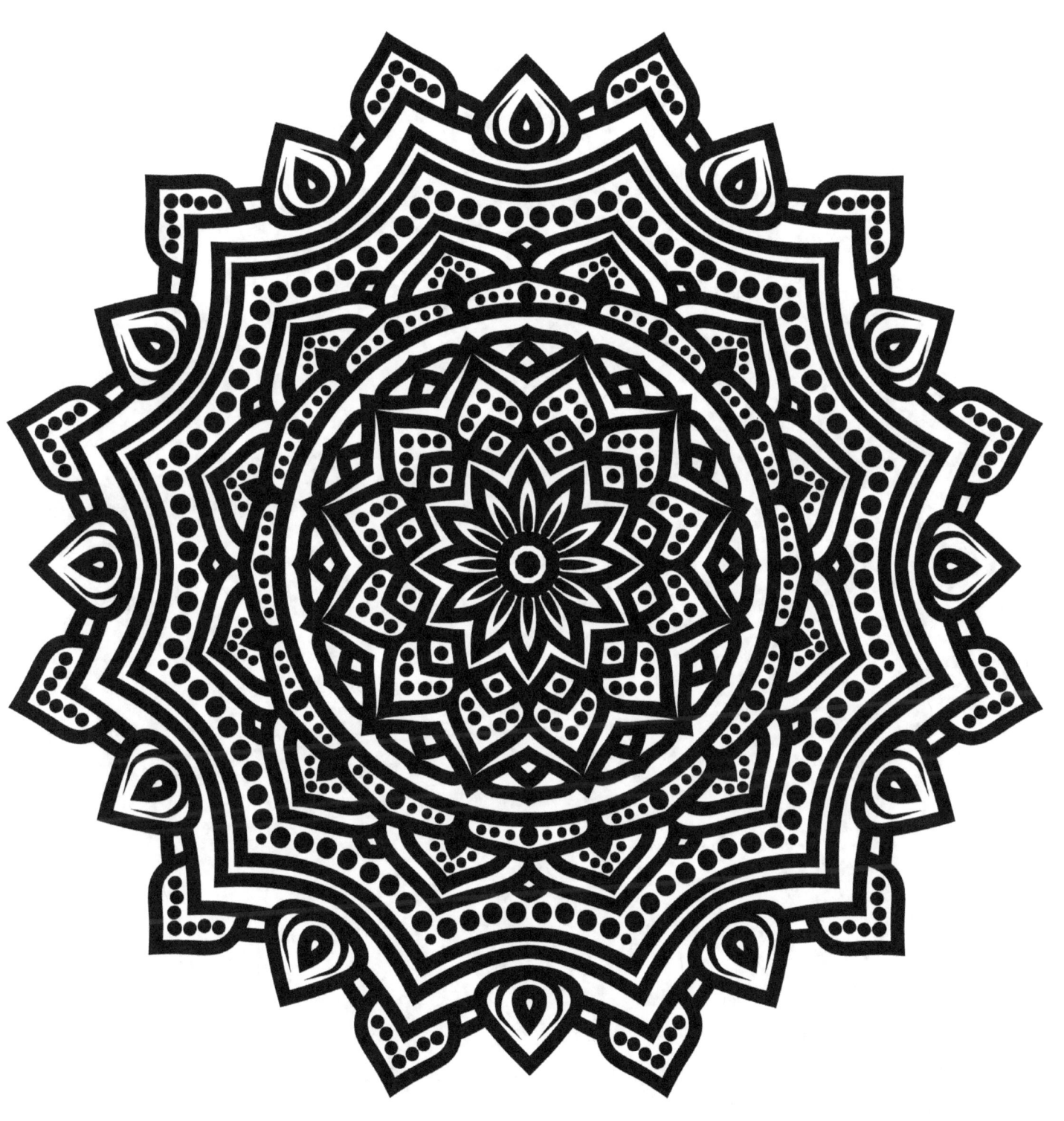

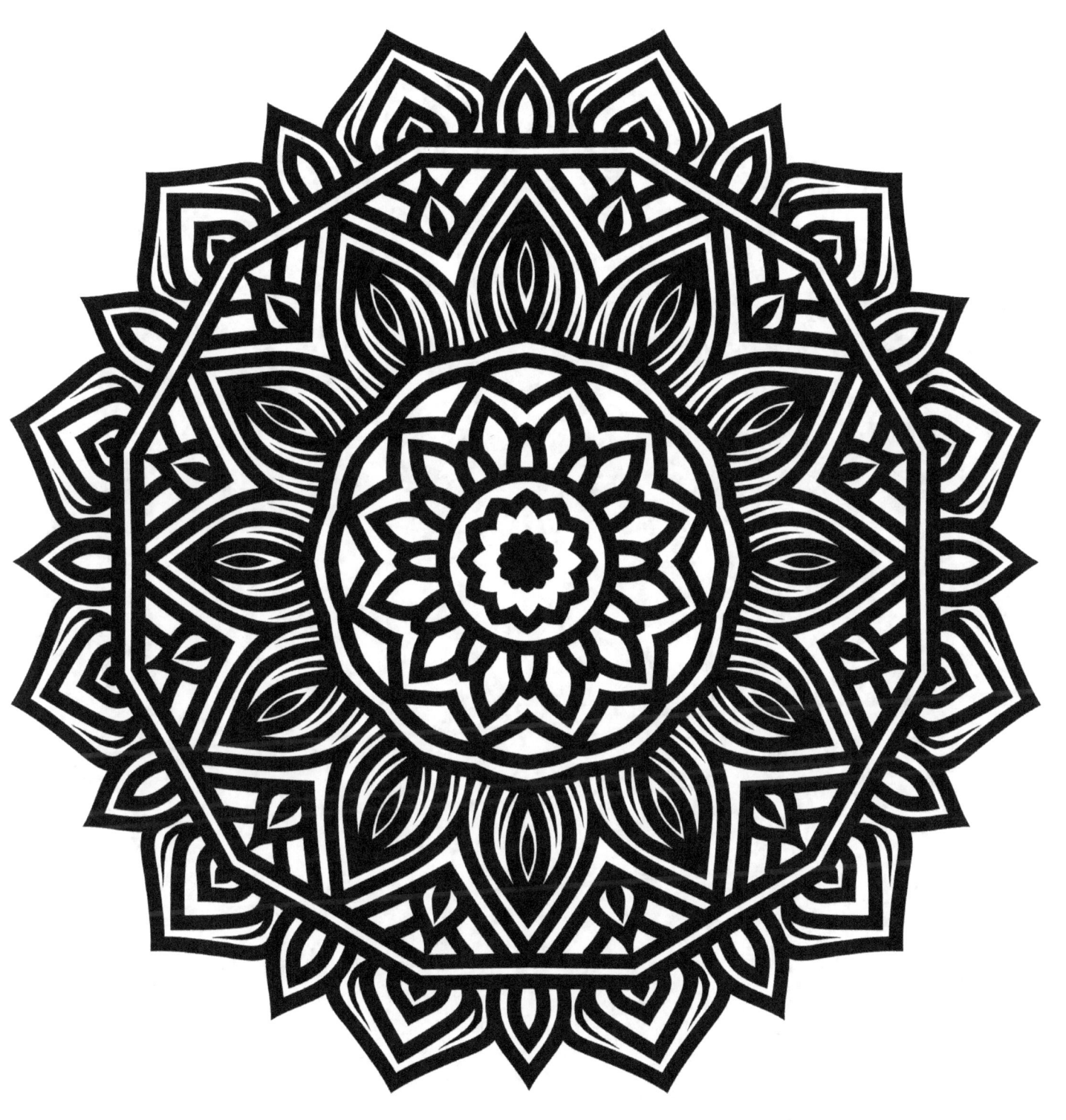

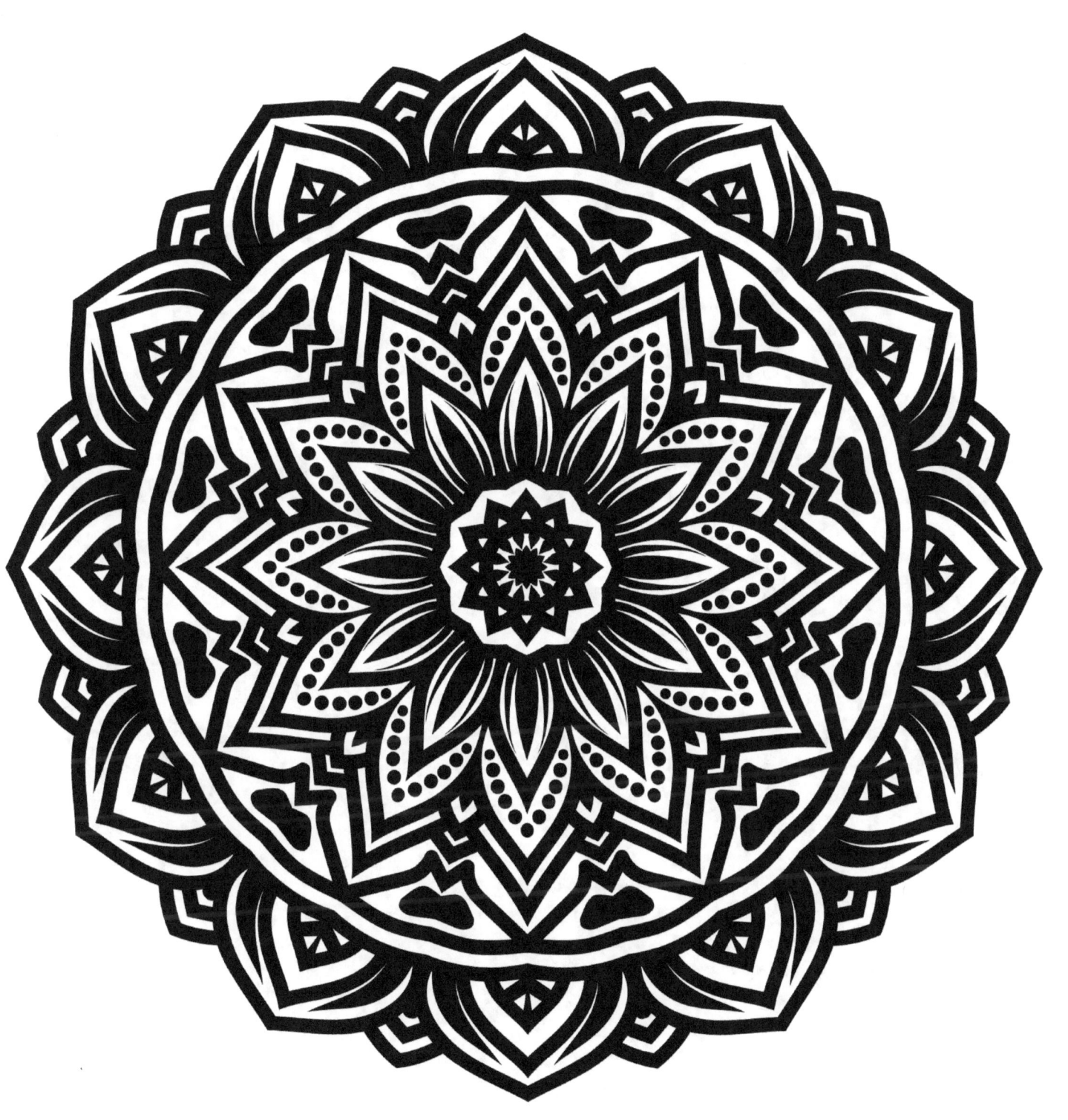

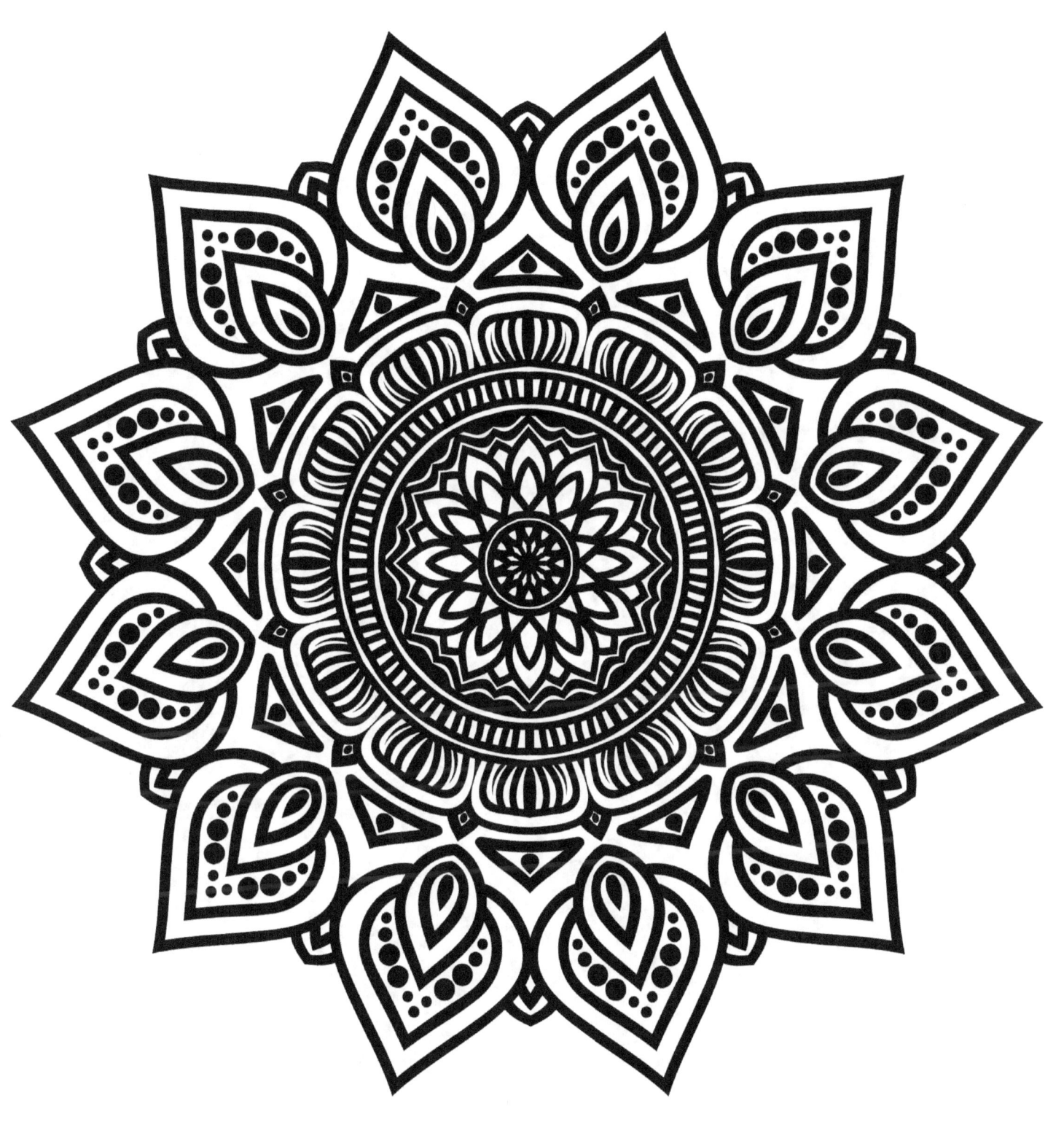

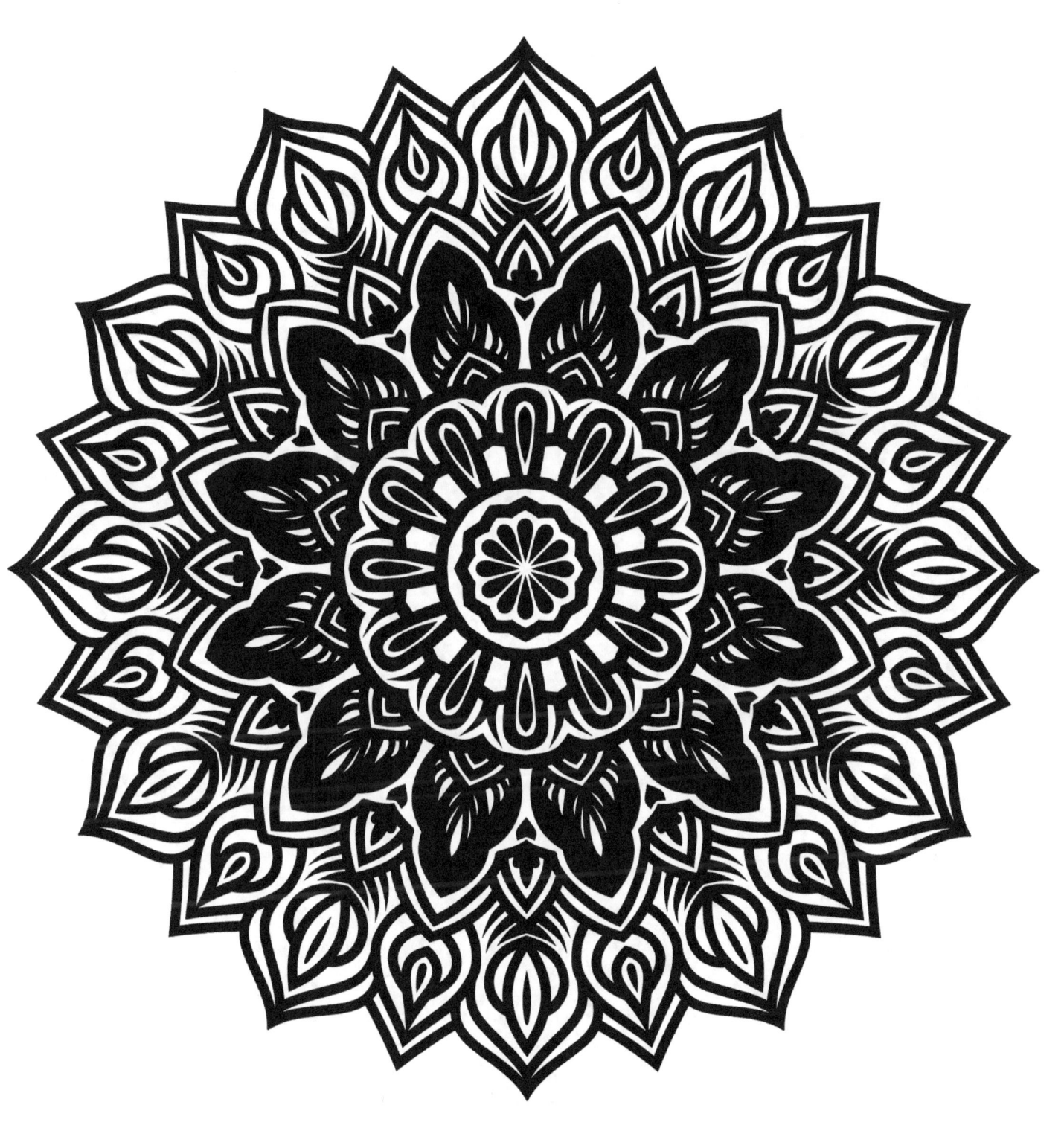

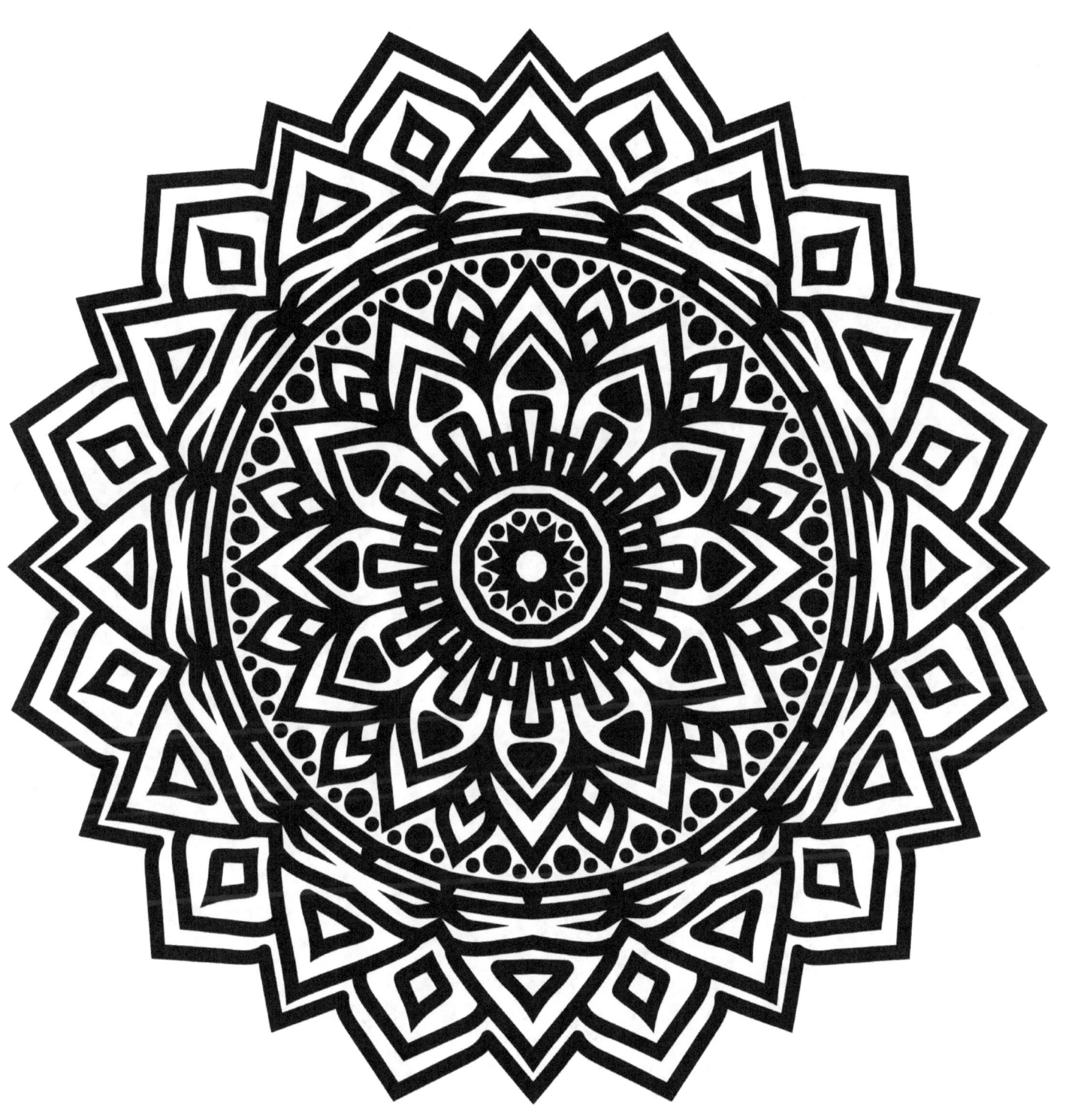

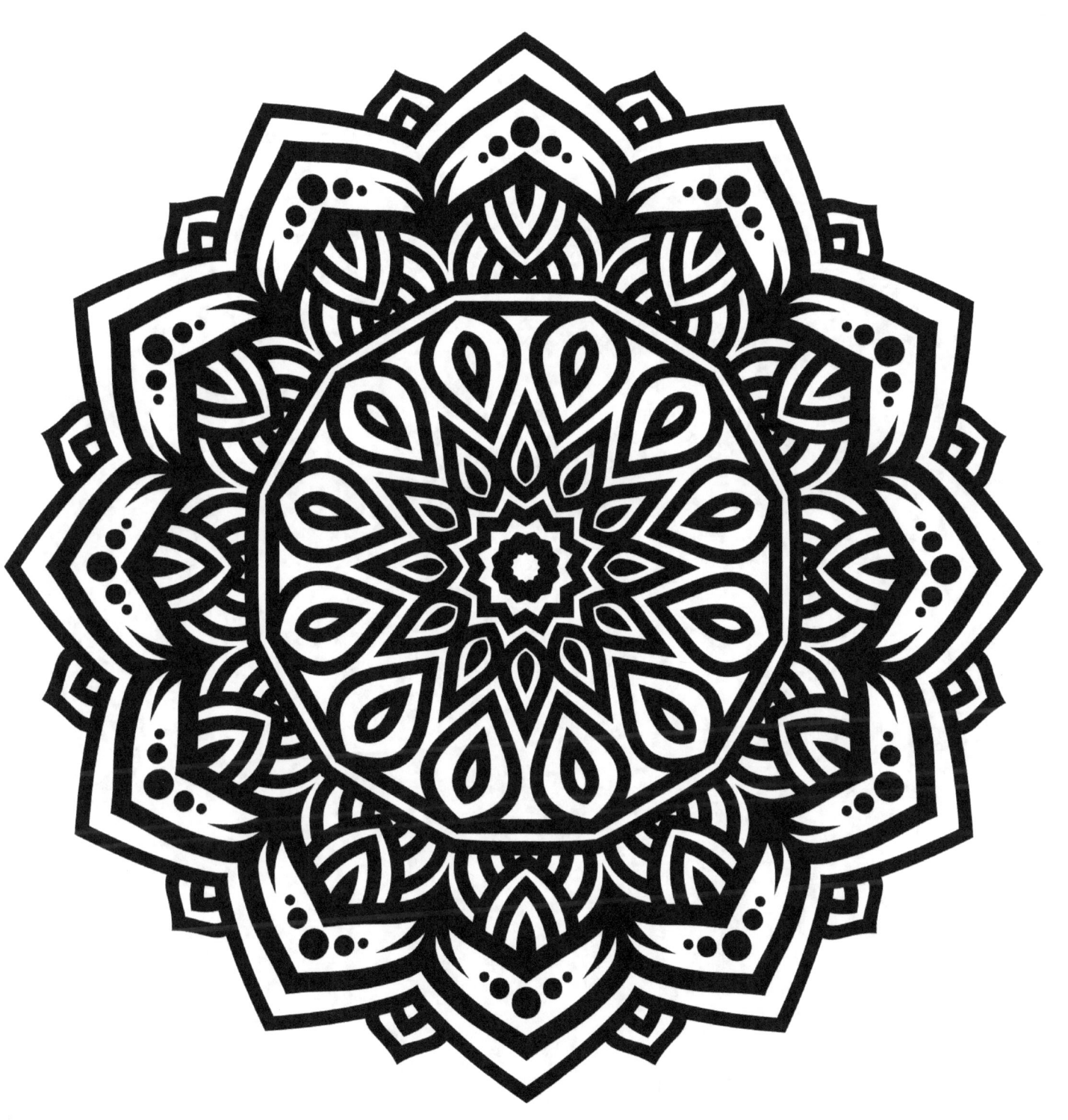

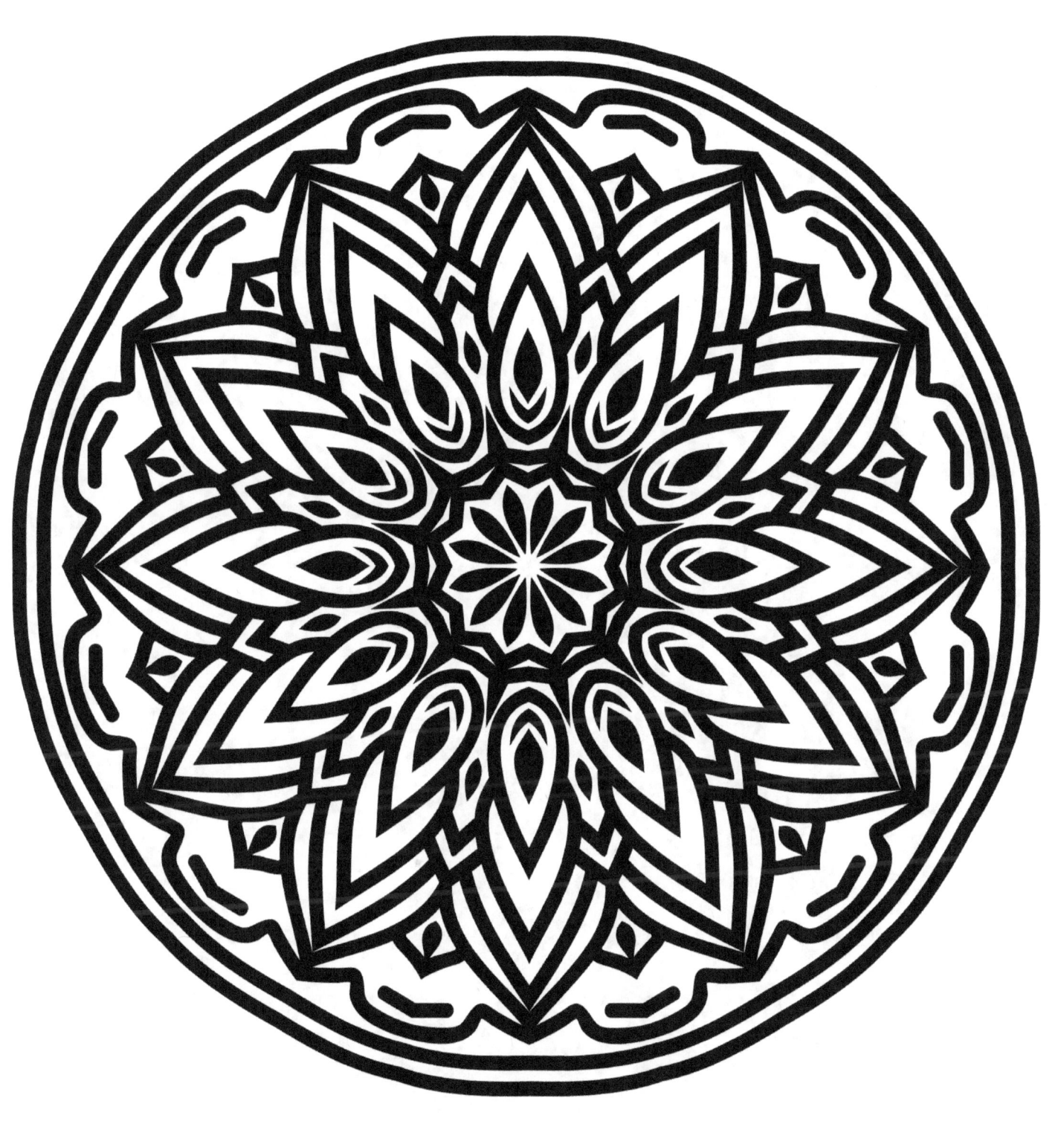

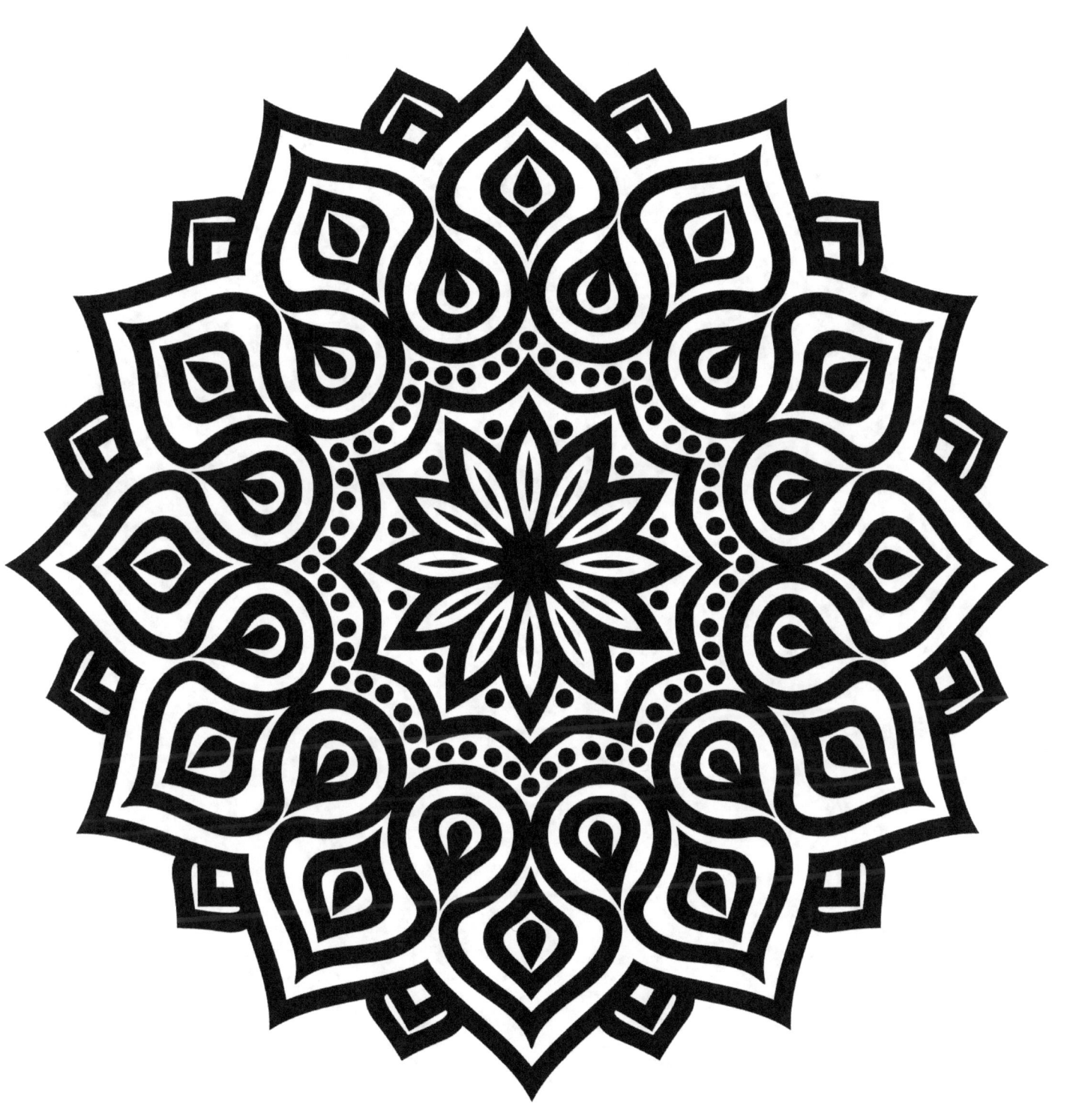

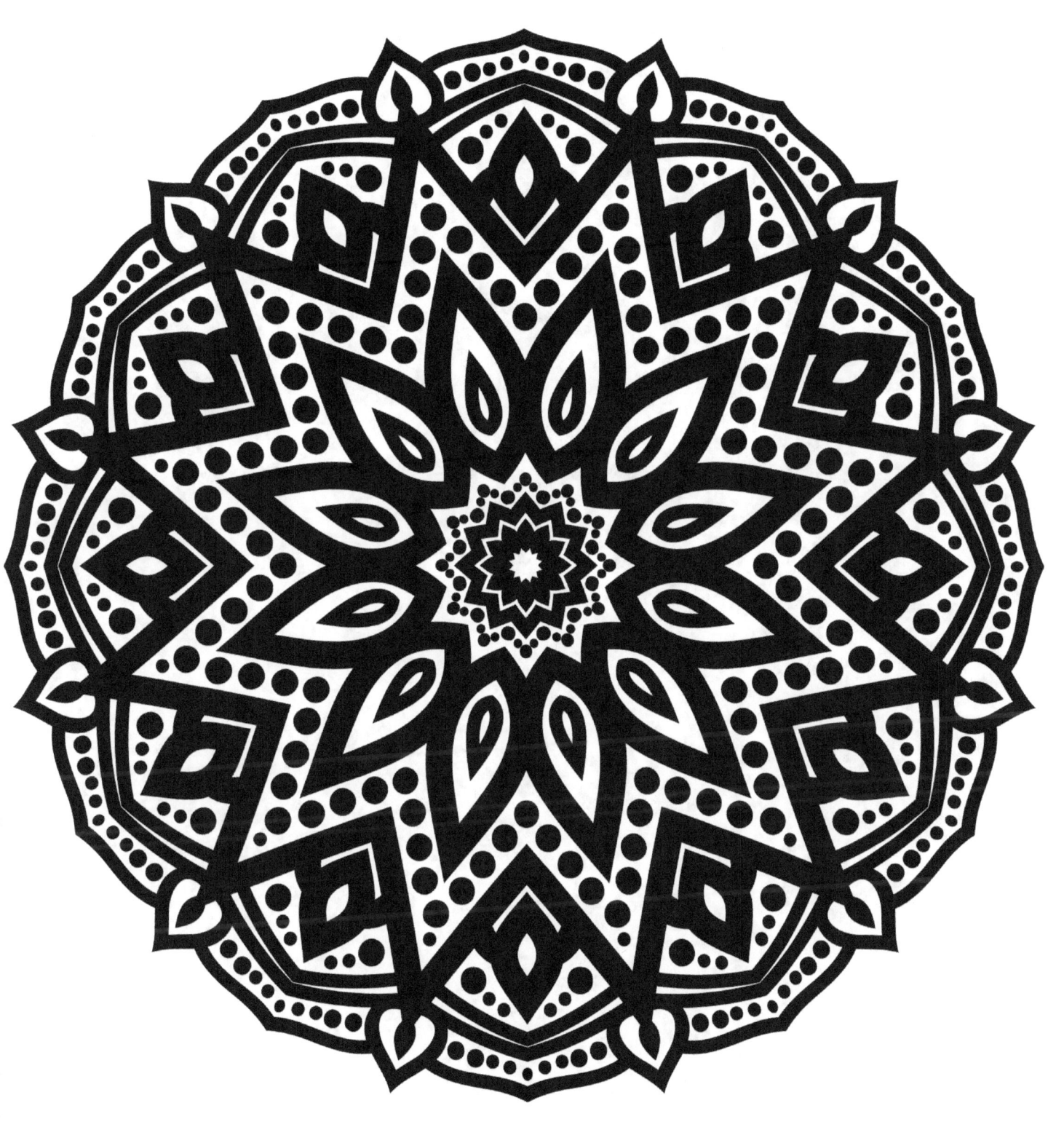

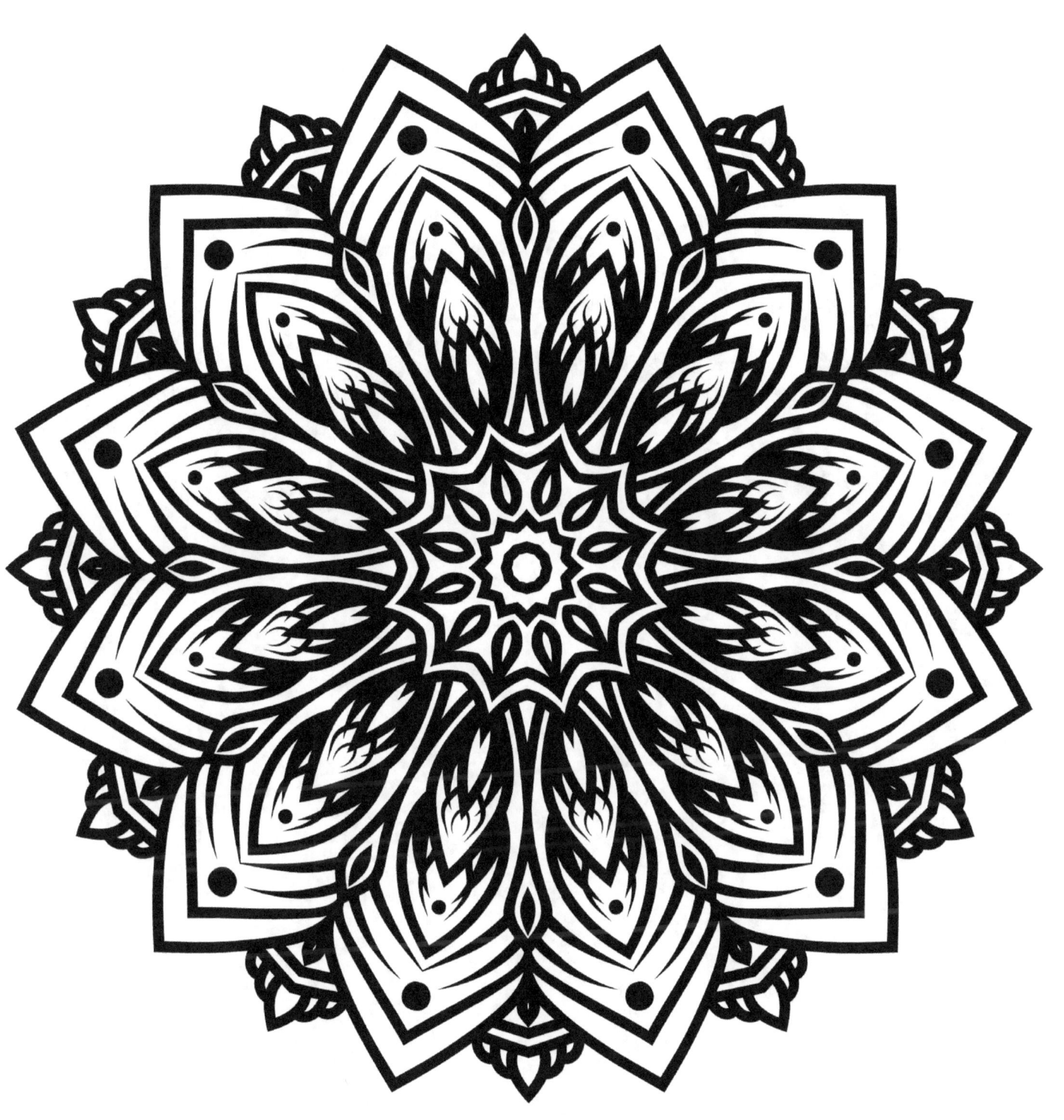

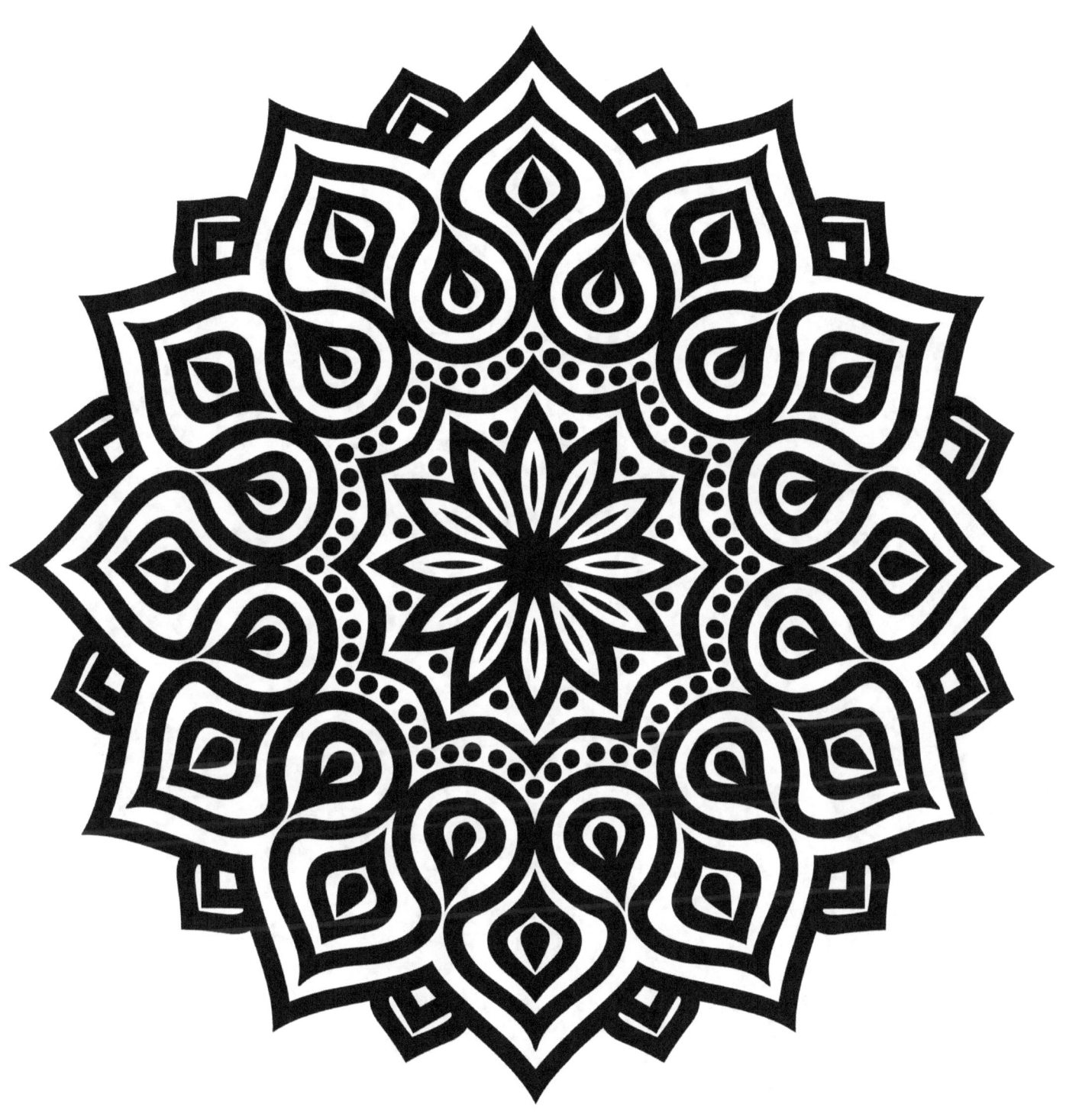

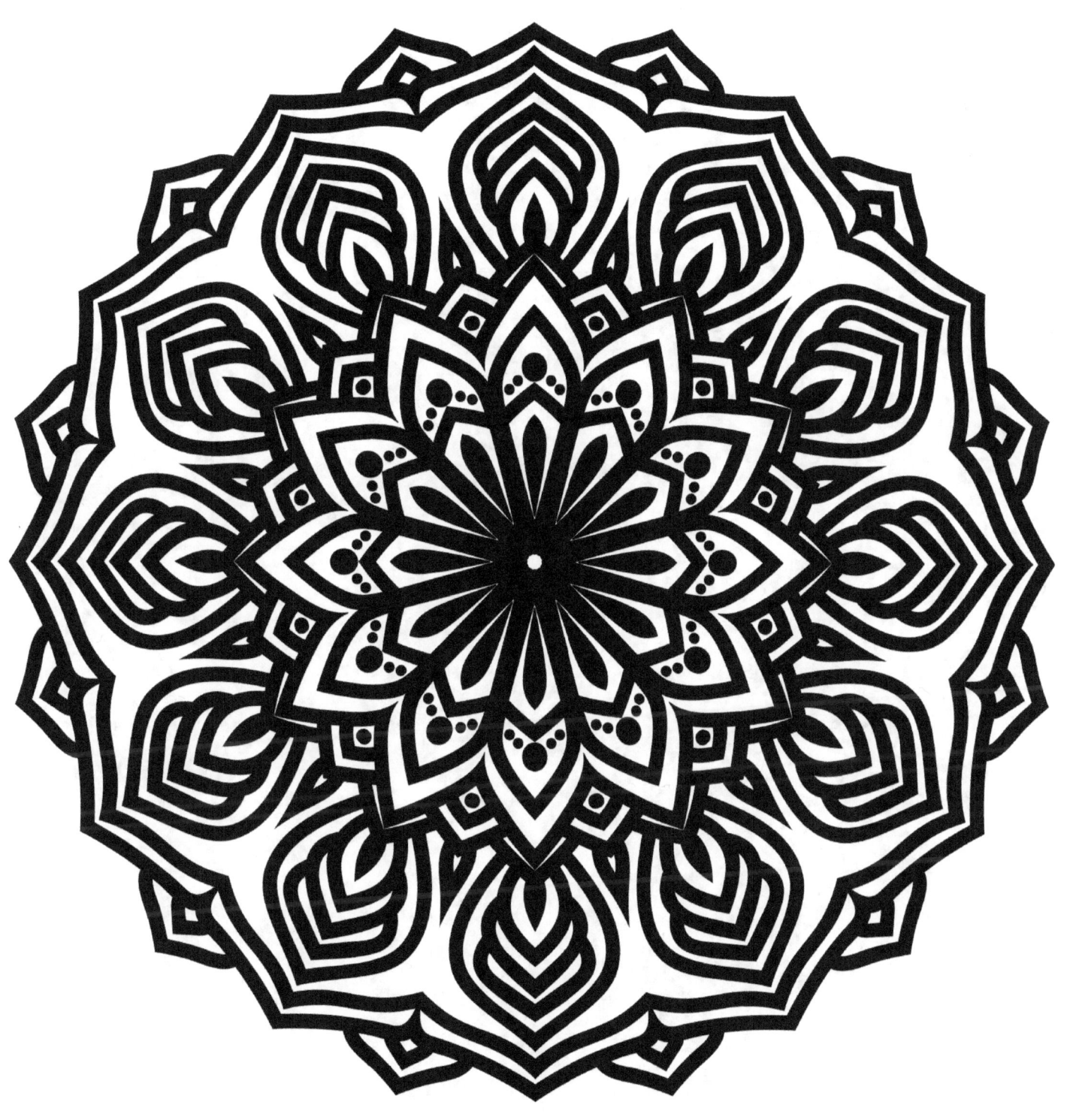

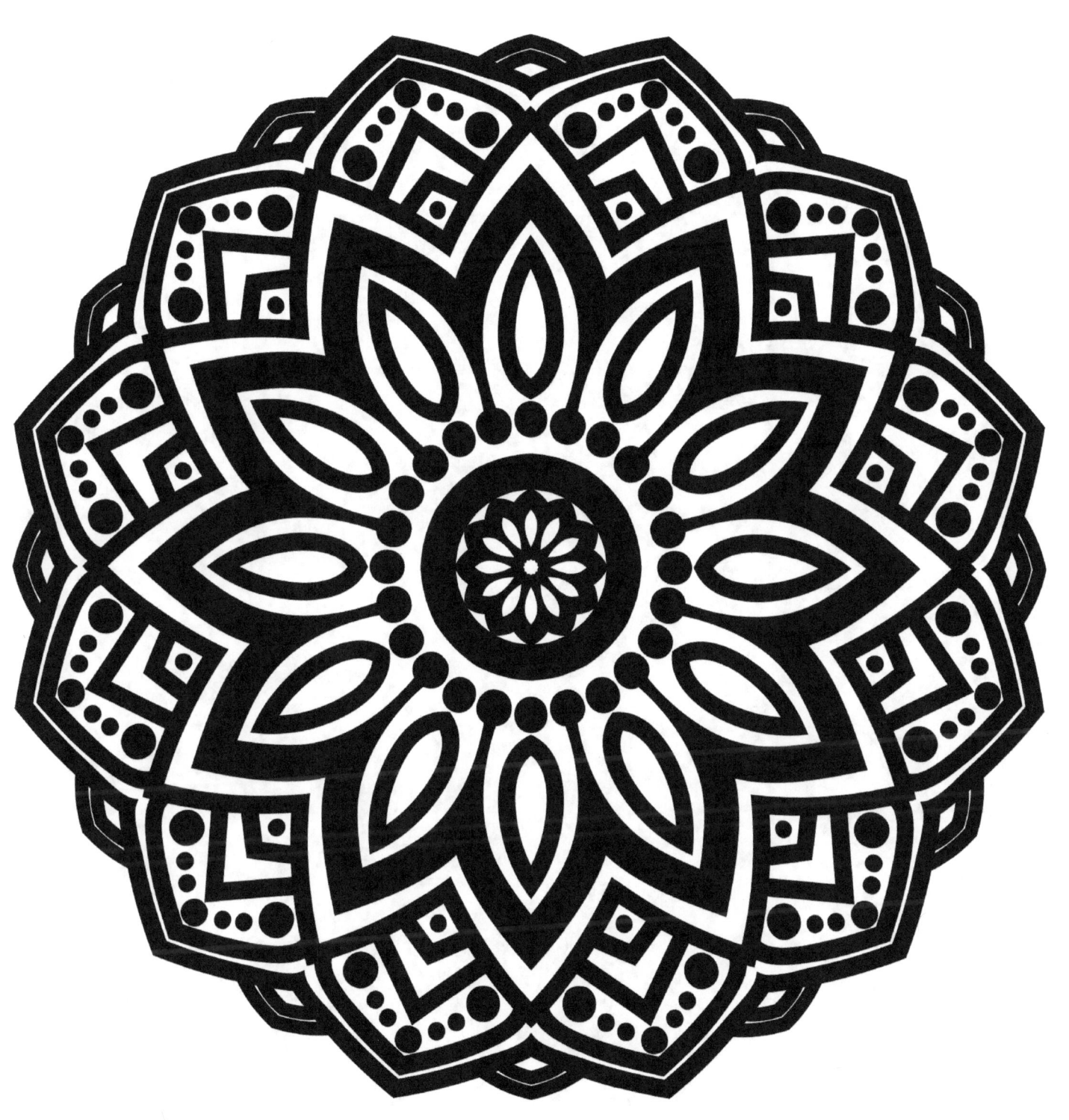

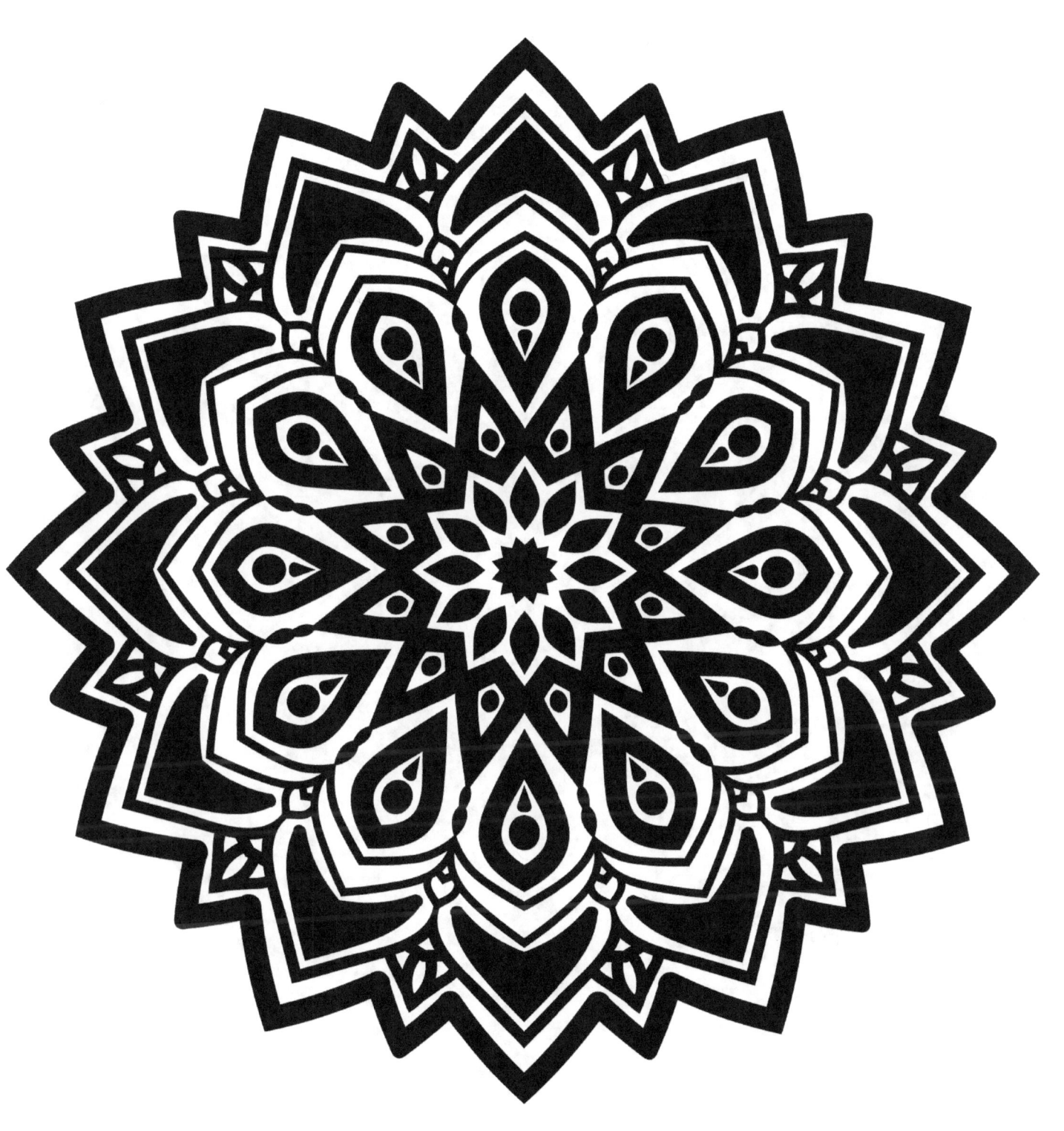

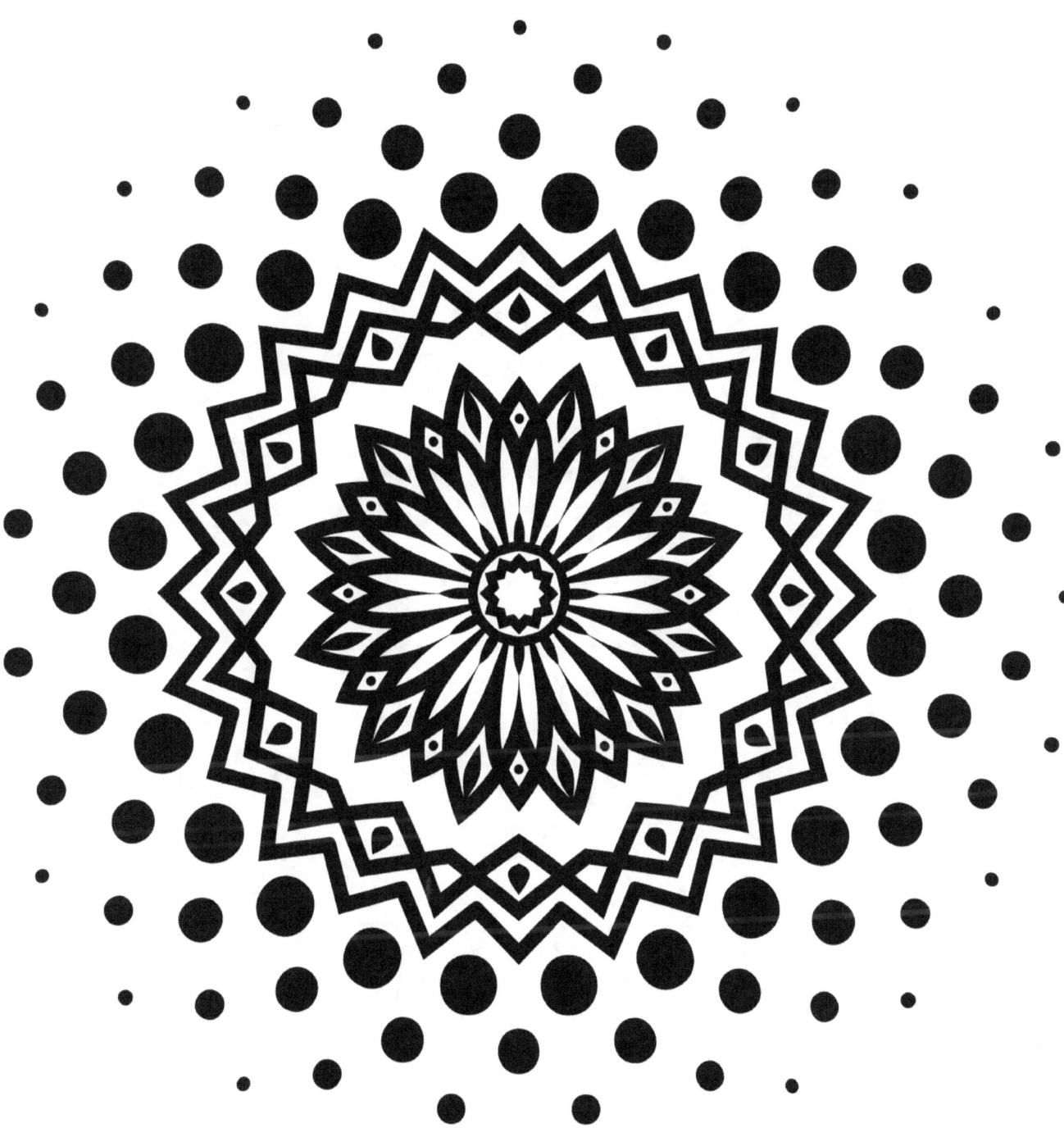

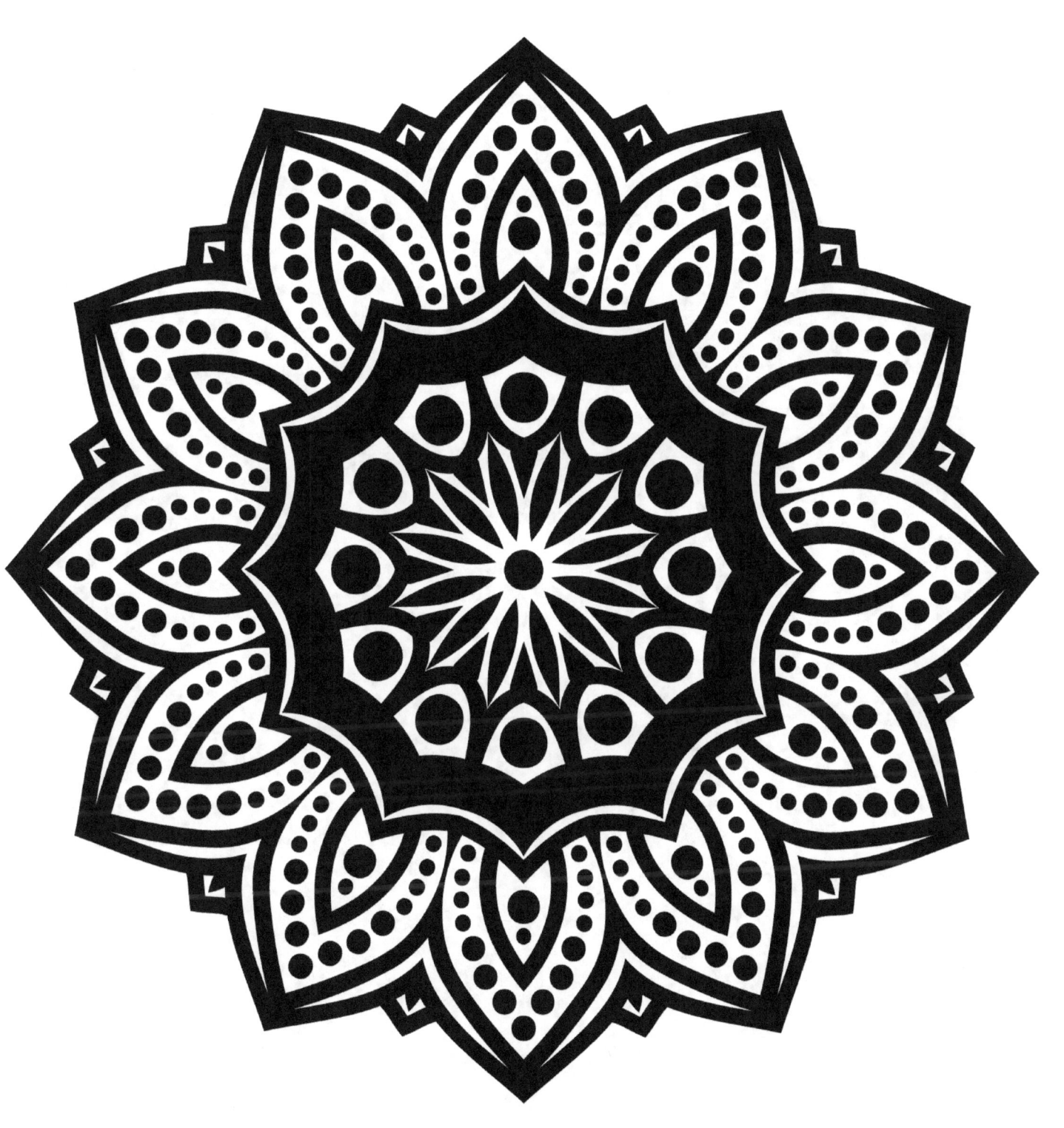

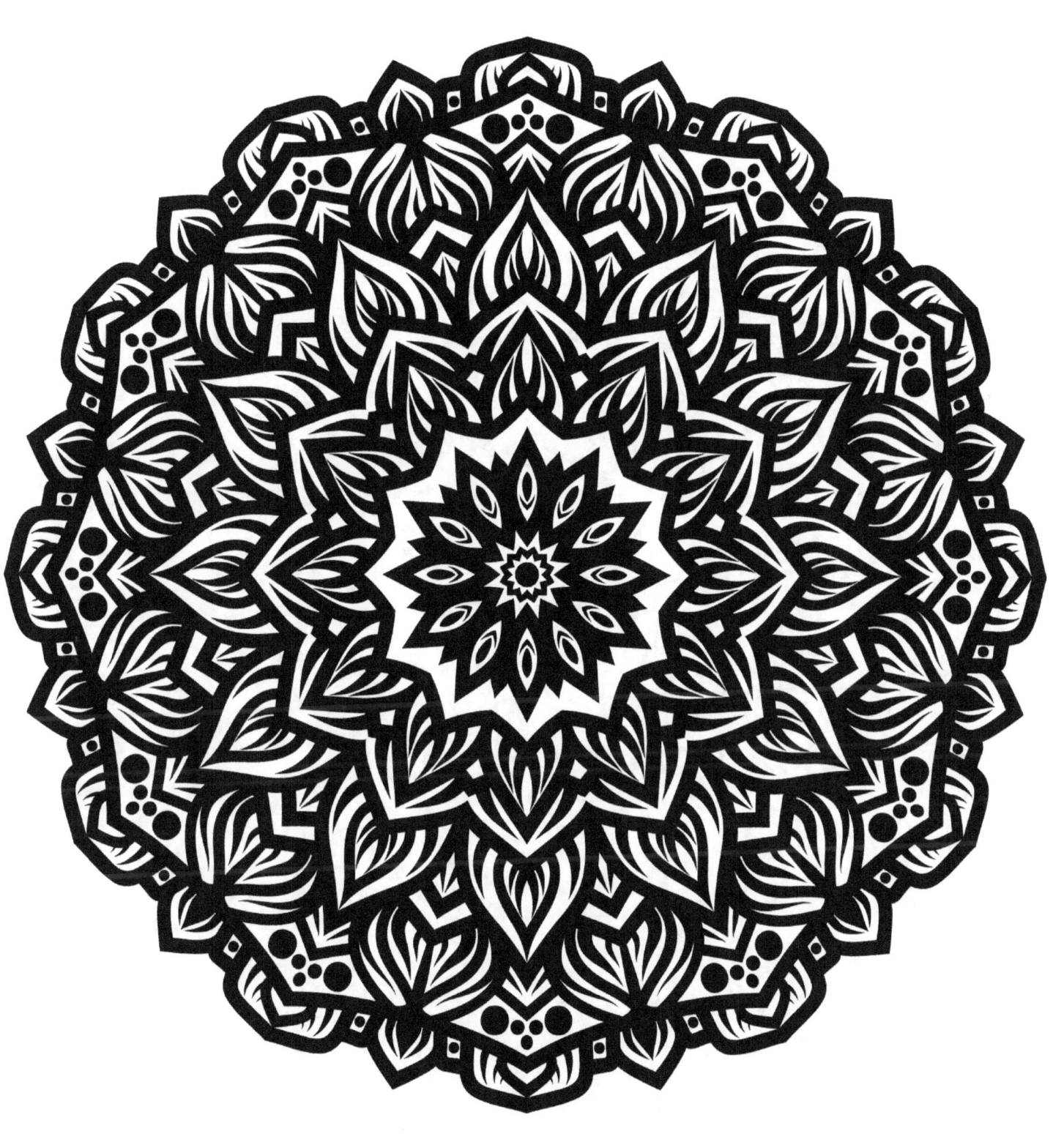

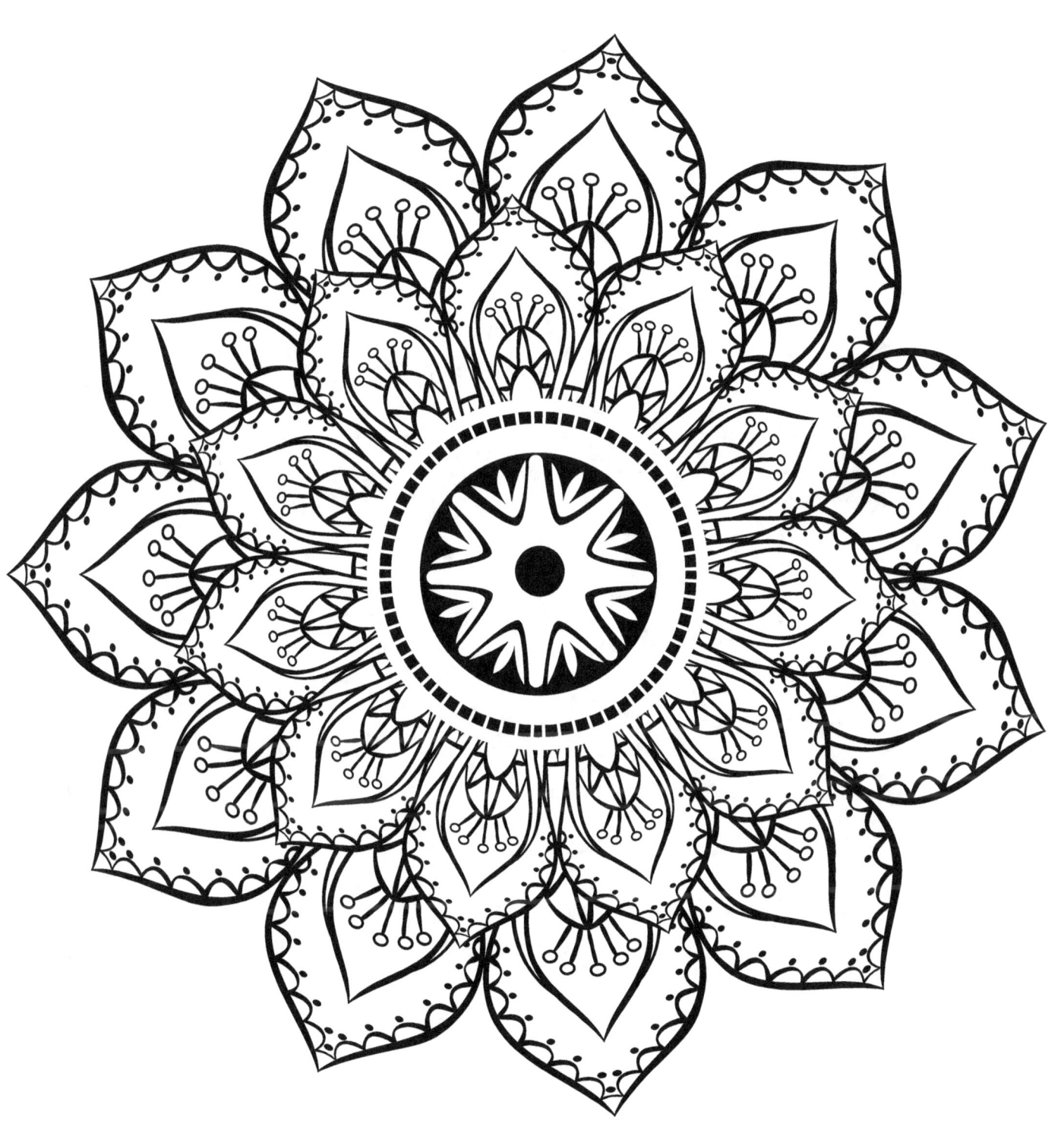

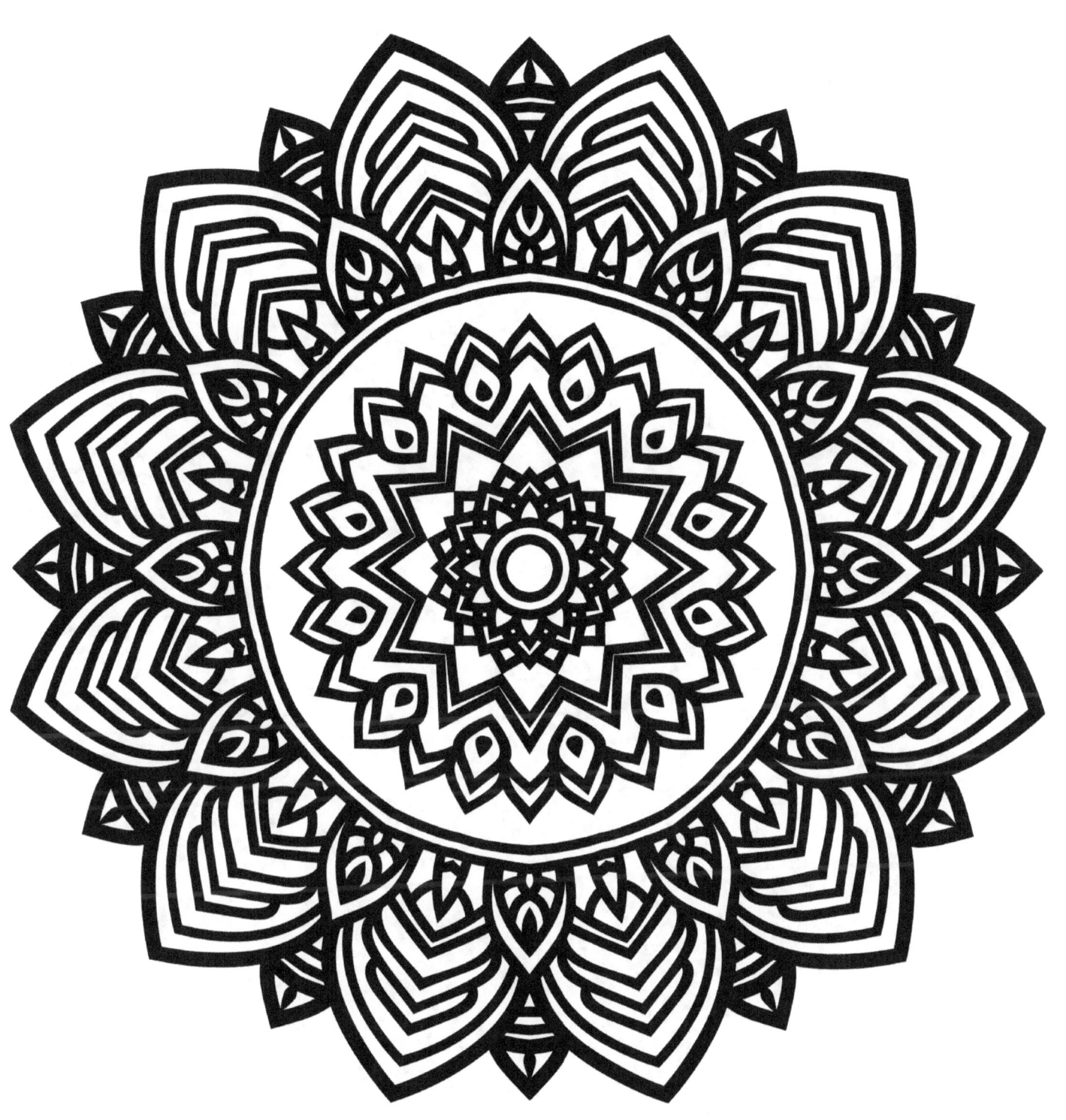

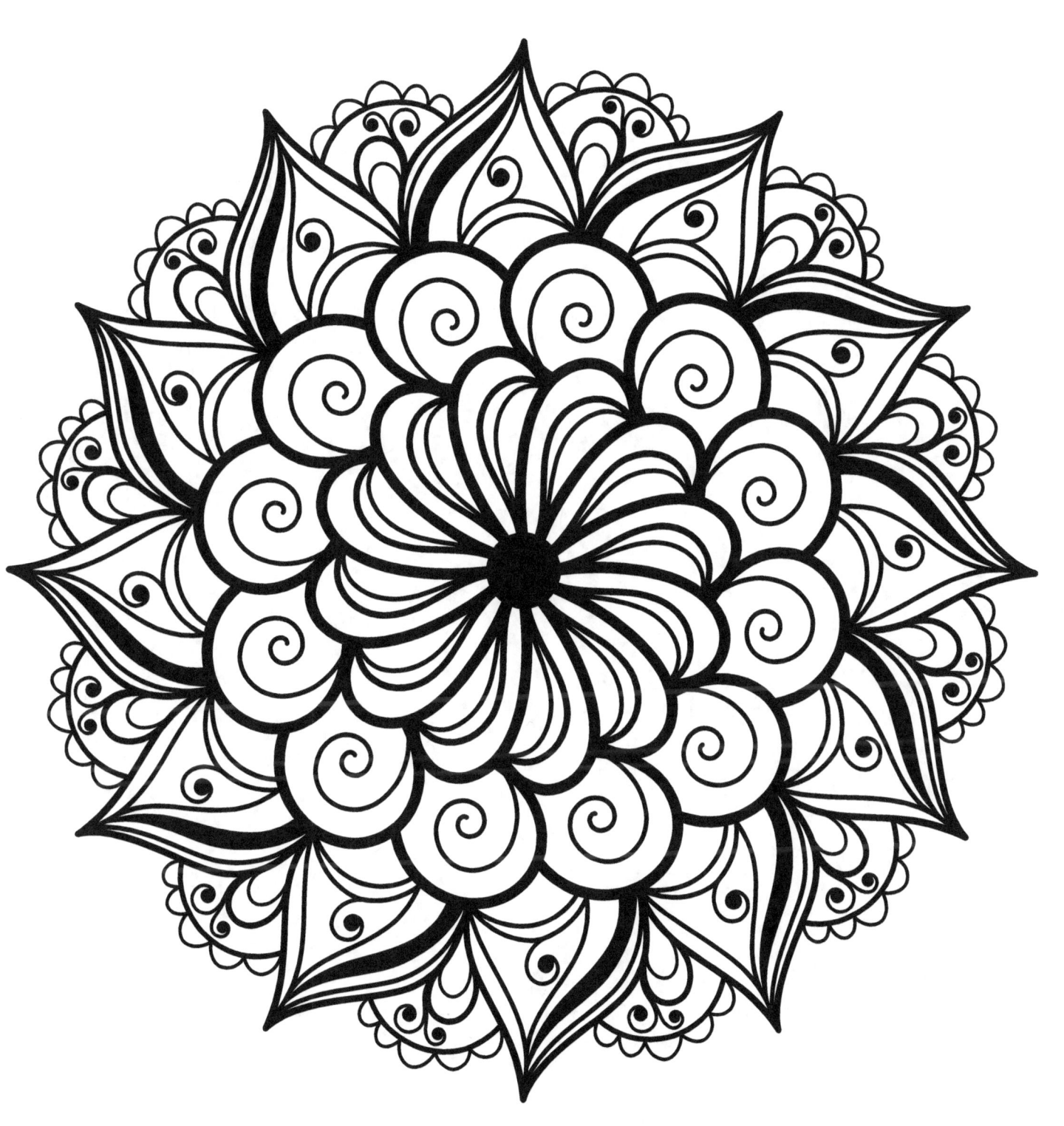

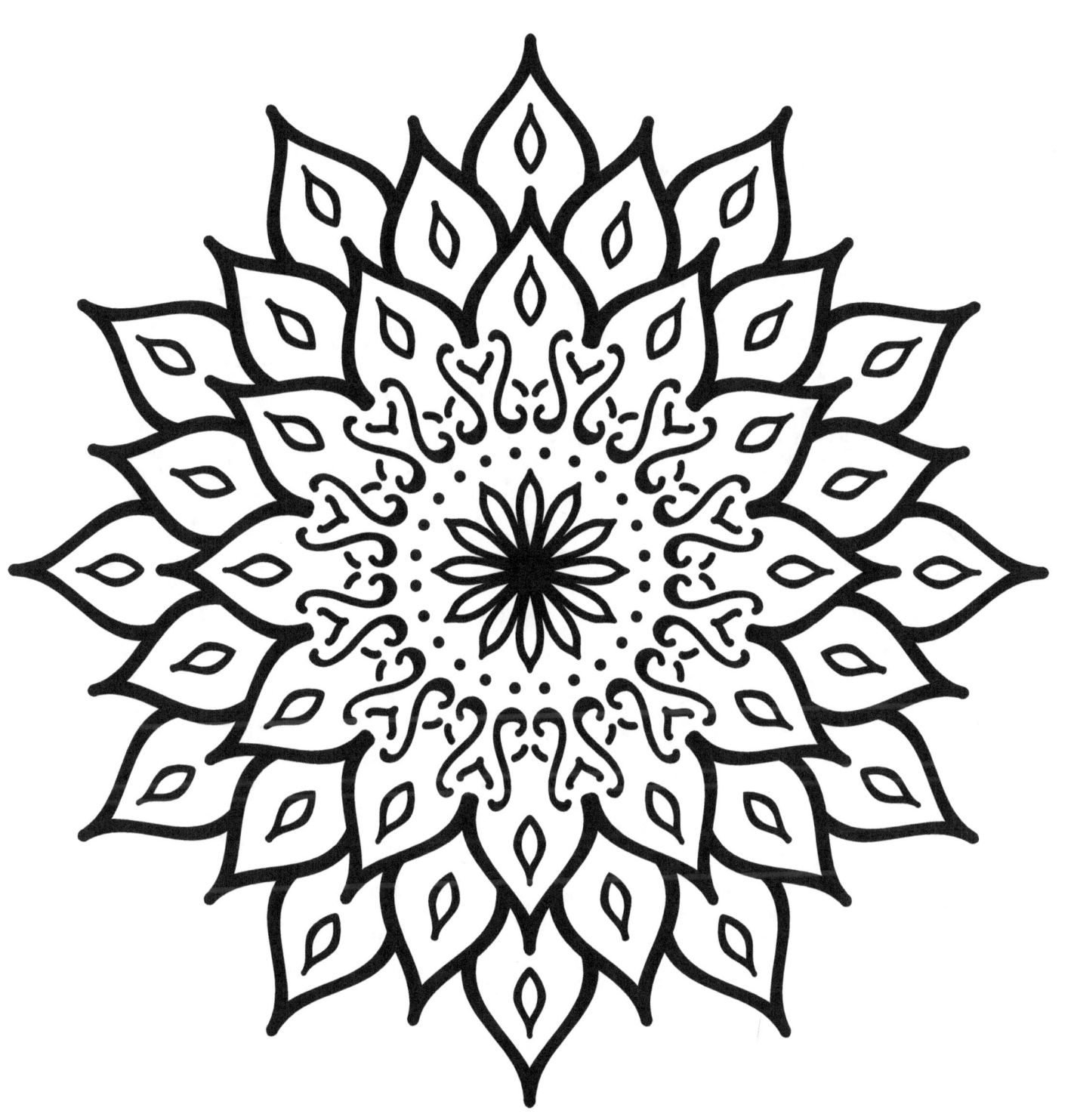

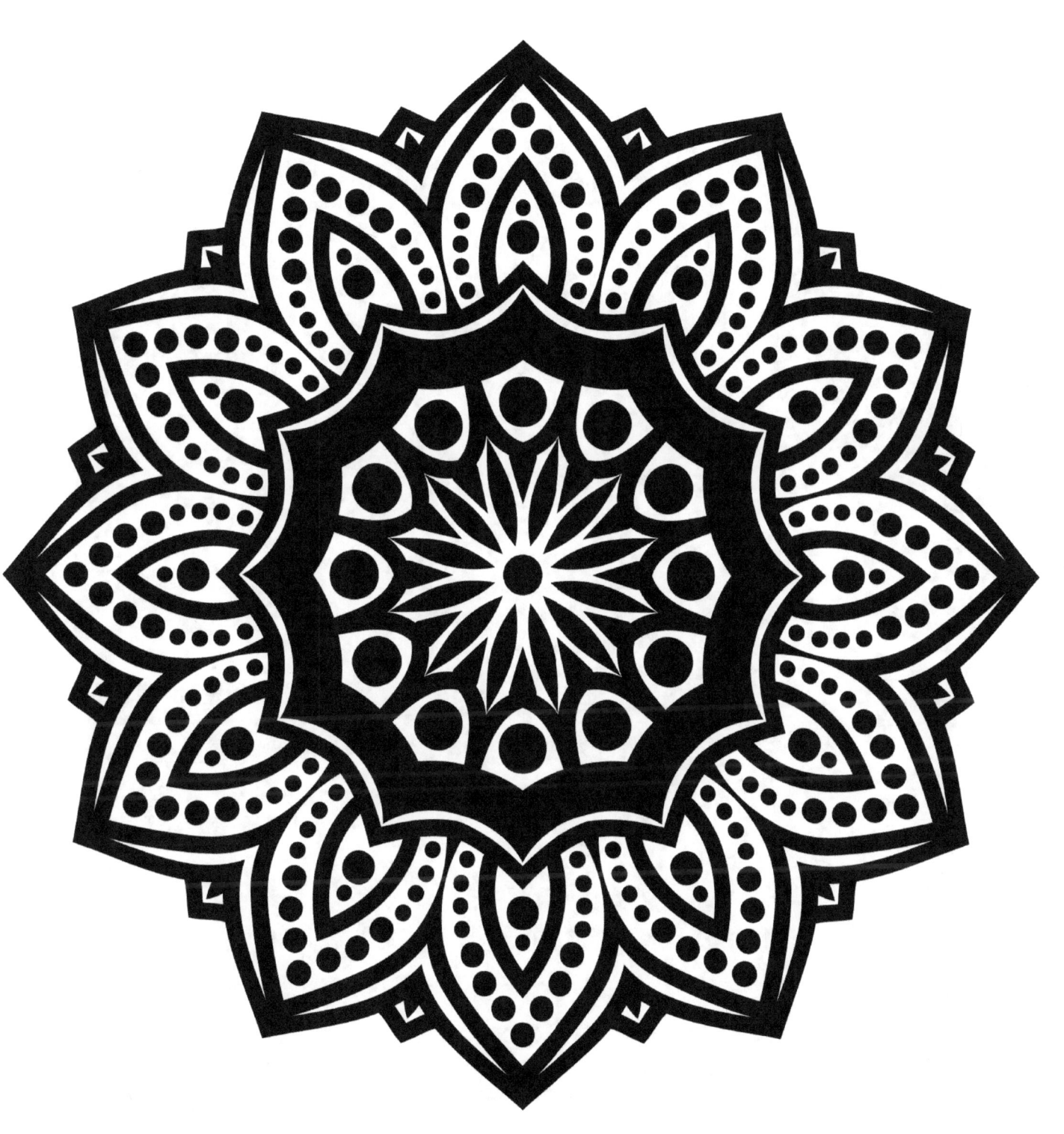

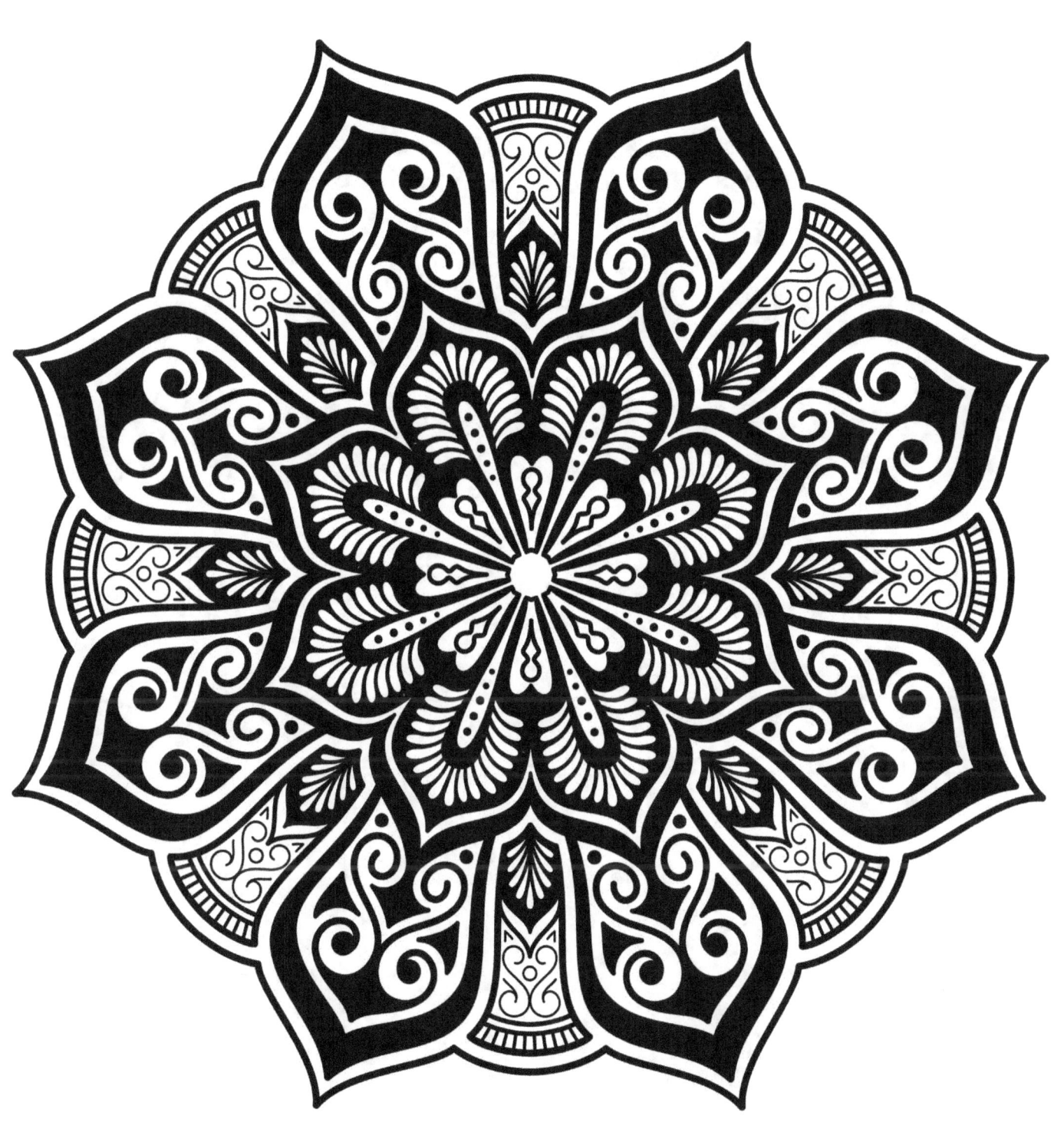

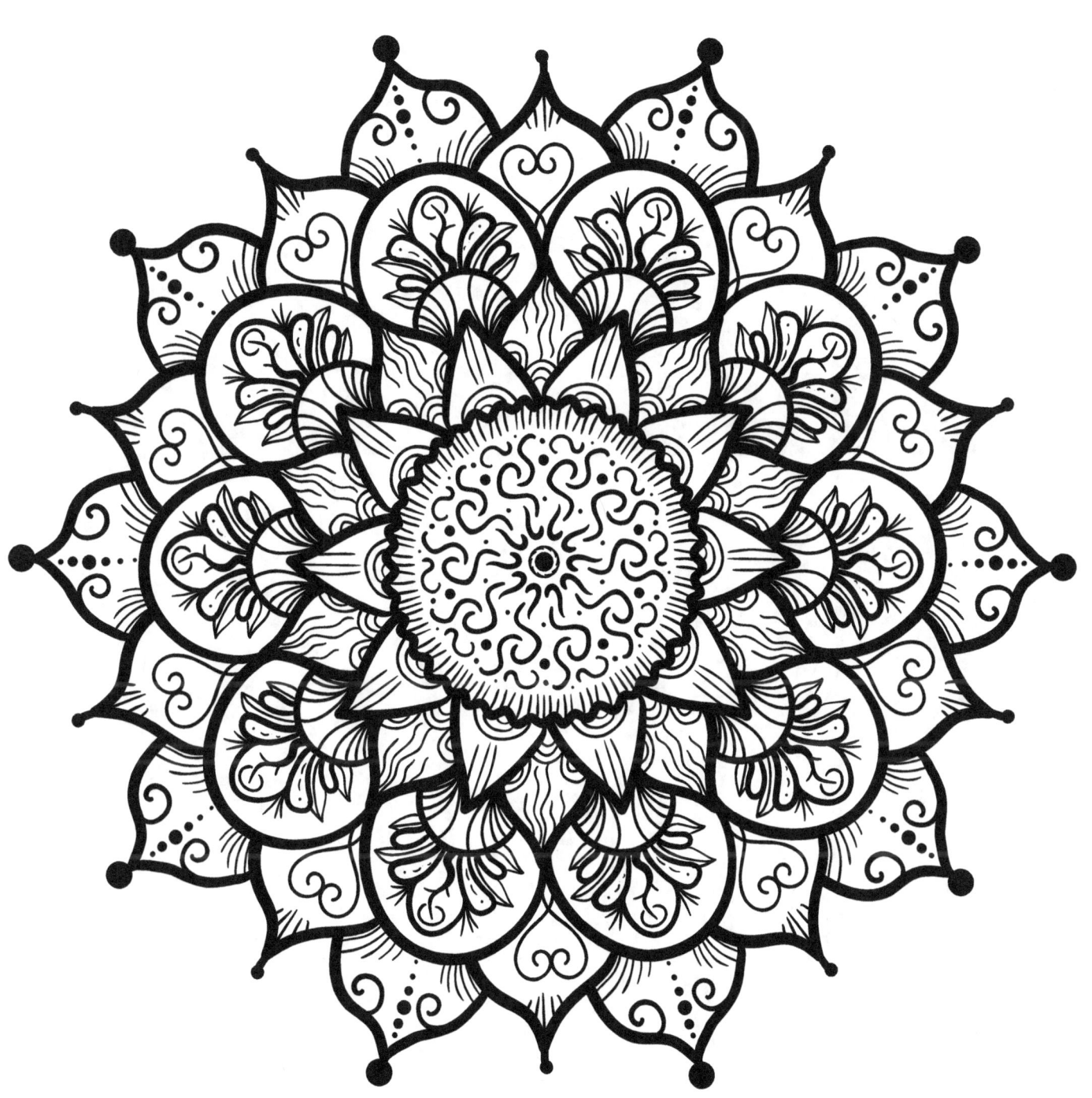

www.ingramcontent.com/pod-product-compliance
Lightning Source LLC
Chambersburg PA
CBHW081446220526
45466CB00008B/2531